To Pam —
Remember God has all the strength + all the answers!
Love
Becky

STRENGTH IN TIMES OF TROUBLE

by

Lea Fowler

D1606335

All Biblical quotations are taken from the New American Standard Version unless otherwise noted.

Copyright 1989 © Lea Fowler

ISBN: 0-89137-455-8

DEDICATED TO:

The One who showed us how to suffer.

GRATITUDE TO:

Becky, my daughter, who "mid-wifed" this book to delivery. I doubt that it would have survived without her help.

FELLOW SUFFERERS

The Loss of a Child	Church Problems
Holland & Gladys B.	*Duane & Betty B.*
Alex & Millie G.	*John & Jackie B.*
Hulen & Etta M.	*Tom & Linda F.*
Gerald & Ann N.	*Randy & Sharon G.*
Bruce & Sherry P.	*Bill & Beverly H.*
Jim & Kathy T.	*Herb & Ila M.*
Charles & Kay W.	*Russ & Jean M.*

And a special friend who suffered; she knows who she is.

A special thank you to Russ, who endured the writing of another book with love and encouragement.

FOREWORD

Suffering is a part of every Christian life. It has its own peculiar purpose—God-sent or God-allowed, for our own good. "Must Jesus bear the cross alone and all the world go free? No, there's a cross for everyone—and there's a cross for me."

QUALITY PUBLICATIONS
P.O. BOX 7385
FT. WORTH, TX 76111

INTRODUCTION

It takes a long time to understand the benefits of suffering. It takes probably even longer to learn to live a joyful life while suffering. It takes a strong faith to continue to believe that *whatever* it is, God will cause it to work together for good.

TABLE OF CONTENTS

FOR IT IS INEVITABLE
Chapter 1

"Why do you teach so much about suffering?" a good friend once asked me. "I have never suffered," she continued.
"You will," I answered, and she has, and she still is.

Why Come To Earth?

Paul Harvey tells a modern parable about a religious skeptic who worked as a farmer. It seems that one raw winter night the man heard an irregular thumping against the kitchen storm door. He went to the window and watched as tiny, shivering sparrows attracted to the evident warmth inside, beat in vain against the glass.

Touched, the farmer bundled up and trudged through fresh snow to open the barn door for the struggling birds. He turned on the lights and tossed some hay in the corner. But the sparrows, which had scattered in all directions when he emerged from the house, hid in the darkness, afraid.

The man tried various tactics to get them into the barn. He laid down a line of saltine cracker crumbs to direct them. He tried circling behind the birds to drive them toward the barn. Nothing worked. Him being a huge alien creature—had terrified them; the birds couldn't comprehend that he actually desired to help.

The farmer withdrew to the house and watched the doomed sparrows through a window. As he stared, a thought hit him like lightning from a clear blue sky: If only I could become a bird—one of them—for just a moment. Then I wouldn't frighten them so. I could show them the way to warmth and safety.

At the same moment another thought dawned on him. He grasped the reason Jesus was born.

He became a sparrow, too, one of us. And that's the way we survive our sufferings. He came to earth and showed us the way to survive. "Many are the afflictions of the righteous but the Lord delivers him out of them all" (Psalm 34:19).

Our self-esteem should come from God loving us—even in our sins—and from Jesus loving us enough to suffer in our place.

It was prophesied in Isaiah 53:4-12, 750 years before it happened, that Christ would bear our griefs and carry our sorrows. He would be pierced through for our transgressions—crushed for our sins. We would be healed by His scourging. God was pleased to crush Him to give mankind a way back, and Christ just poured Himself out to death (Isaiah 53:4-12).

"No temptation has overtaken you but such as is common to man; and God is faithful, who will not allow you to be tempted beyond what you are able, but with the temptation will provide the way of escape also, that you may be able to endure it" (1 Corinthians 10:13).

This is a promise made by God to His children. Whatever you are experiencing, you will NOT bear it alone nor will the load be too heavy.

"I will never desert you nor forsake you, so that we confidently say, 'The Lord is my helper, I will not be afraid, what shall man do to me?' " (Hebrews 13:5-6)

Satan remarked to God concerning Job, "Why shouldn't Job follow you—you have a fence around him" (Job 1:10). And, we, too, can have that same fence around us!

God limits Satan to just how far he can go with us! He prowls outside the fence, hoping we will venture out. He dangles his toys and pleasures and tries to entice us to leave the sheep-fold of safety so that he can pounce on us and devour us.

But the Shepherd knows Satan's ways and is ever on guard for our good—for our soul's safety.

Did you know that it is still the custom of many shepherds when they have a wandering sheep to break a back leg of that sheep? Then the shepherd places the wounded sheep on the back of his own neck and carries it until the bone is healed. That sheep never strays again. It has learned through its suffering the comfort and love of the shepherd. The sheep has learned to trust his shepherd.

And, we, too, must have our legs broken, in a sense, so that we may suffer and learn the comfort and love of our Shepherd. We have to learn where our strength really is. It is not in mankind. "The arm of flesh will fail us and we dare not trust our own," an old hymn says. Hopefully, we, too, become like the sheep that has learned its lesson, and we no longer desire to leave the Shepherd's side.

Do We Have To Suffer?

No, really we don't. It's a choice.

You have not yet resisted to the point of shedding blood in your striving against sin; and you have forgotten the exhortation which is addressed to you as sons, "My son, do not regard lightly the discipline of the Lord, nor faint when you are reproved by him; for those whom the Lord loves he disciplines, and he scourges every son whom his father receives." It is for discipline that your endure; God deals with you as with sons; for what son is there whom his father does not discipline? But if you are without discipline, of which all have become partakers, then you are illegitimate children and not sons. Furthermore, we had earthly fathers to discipline us, and we respected them; shall we not much rather be subject to the Father of spirits, and live? For they disciplined us for a short time as seemed best to them, but He disciplines for our good that we may share His holiness. All discipline for the moment seems not to be joyful, but sorrowful; yet to those who have been trained by it, afterwards it yields the peaceful fruit of righteousness.

Hebrews 12:4-9

Discipline is the Father's business, just as it is parents' business. We don't discipline the child who lives next door—he is not our responsibility.

But, we *can* refuse to walk the narrow path. We can change our allegiance from God's care and teaching to "doing it our way." Though "the way of the transgressor is hard," it is still the free way—the broad way, the way of the grasshopper who is not mindful of the coming cold of winter (or the heat of eternity).

In the parable of the sower (Matthew 13:3-9, 18-23), there was one group made of shallow soil. This represented those who heard the word with gladness and excitement. They bloomed quickly, but when the sun got hot and the suffering came, they quit because "they had no root in themselves."

Moses *chose* to suffer—he weighed the matter carefully. Shall I stay the grandson of Pharaoh or endure ill treatment with the people of God? (Hebrews 11:24-25). "He considered the reproach of Christ greater riches than the treasures of Egypt, for he was looking to the reward" (Hebrews 11:26).

Joshua said, "And if it's disagreeable in your sight to serve the Lord, *choose* for yourselves today whom you will serve. Whether the gods which your fathers served which are beyond the River, or the gods of the Amorites in whose land you are living, but as for me and my house, we will serve the Lord" (Joshua 24:15).

("And Israel served the Lord all the days of Joshua and all the days

3

of the elders who survived Joshua, and had known all the deeds of the Lord which He had done for Israel" Joshua 24:31).

Our "choosing" to suffer helps others to make the same choice and vice versa. Jesus *chose* suffering because of the joy set before Him. Hebrews 12:2 says, "Fixing our eyes on Jesus, the author and perfecter of our faith, who for the joy set before him endured the cross, despising the shame, and has sat down at the right hand of the throne of God."

Jesus knew how wonderful heaven was! He knew who He was, where He was, and where He was going. We, too, should know who we are, where we are (in the world but not a part of it), and where we are going—home.

Two Classes Of Suffering Saints

It seems to me there are two classes who suffer the most. The first group are those who would be the greatest givers—the greatest servants. Through the years I have seen those "special sufferers." I marvel at their control, patience, and kindness.

The second group are the strong-willed, such as the apostle, Peter. God knows our natures, our genes, our raising. HE KNOWS US!

"Trials are medicines which our gracious and wise physician prescribes, because we need them; and He proportions the frequency and weight of them to what the case requires. Let us trust His skill and thank Him for His prescriptions." Newton

A friend of mine says, "When I am disciplined by the Lord, I strive to learn quickly and say, 'That's enough, that's enough, I repent!' "

Sufferings Are Temporary

Suffering becomes bearable. It *has* a purpose. It is in God's hands, and if it is borne, it will change us. *There are many lessons learned by suffering that cannot be learned any other way!*

"If suffering is accepted and lived through, not fought against and refused, then it is completed and becomes transmuted. It is absorbed, and having accomplished its work, it ceases to exist as suffering, and becomes part of our growing selves." Anon.

This statement has helped change my life. There is a process going on in each of us that starts when we are born again, and suffering is a very important part of the process. We will go into details of this procedure as this book unfolds.

"The Lord redeems the soul of his servants; and none of those who take refuge in him will be condemned" (Psalm 34:22).

4

Murphy's Law

Have you ever heard of Murphy's Law
"All that can go wrong—will"?
God warns us there's evil in each day;
Things will go wrong along the way.
How much easier to bear these constant pains
Remembering God daily monitors the appropriate gains
For hanging in there.

Lea Fowler

QUESTIONS FOR DISCUSSION

1. Did Jesus have the choice to suffer or not to suffer? *Yes*

2. Have you known a "special sufferer?" *Yes*

3. Have you recovered from a bad suffering? *Not totally but do we ever really until we get home with God who will make us perfect.*

REJOICE DURING THE PROCESS
Chapter 2

If Christians could really understand all the good results of suffering, they might even learn to welcome the sorrows that are inevitable.

When all kinds of trials and temptations crowd into your lives, my brothers, don't resent them as intruders, but welcome them as friends! Realize that they come to test your faith and to produce in you the quality of endurance. But let the process go on until that endurance is fully developed, and you will find you have become men of mature character, men of integrity with no weak spots.

Phillips Modern English

Welcome Troubles As Friends
James 1:2

They are sent by God for our learning, for our discipline. "For the commandment is a lamp, and teaching is light; and reproofs for discipline are the way of life" (Proverbs 6:23).

God says, "I am sending you a friend to change you, to soften you—or toughen you up." The tests are not enemies or intruders but God-sent teachers and instructors to help us get our diploma.

If the particular problem is Satan sent—a temptation— God has the *last* say. Only God could make *whatever* it is to work for your good. WE DON'T QUOTE ROMANS 8:28 ENOUGH! "And we know that in all things God works for the good of those who love him, who have been called according to his purpose." NIV

"Moreover we know that to those who love God, who are called according to his plans, everything that happens fits into a pattern for good." Phillips

Many misunderstand this verse. They hastily say, "I love God, so everything works for *my* good." But, we must read all the verse. It works together for the saved, those who obey His call.

If we love Him, we will keep all of His commandments. Satan will try to deceive us by telling us if we just are a believer, then we love Him. *Satan is a believer!* (James 2:19)

God sends the trials, and Satan sends the temptations. Sometimes it is difficult to know which is which.

The Trying Of The Gold

Those who would be the greatest servant will probably suffer the most! God tells us that there are all kinds of vessels. "Now if any one builds on the foundation with gold, silver, precious stones, wood, hay, straw—then each man's work will become manifest. . ." (1 Corinthians 3:12).

If we are to become the gold—we must be tried over and over. I've heard it said that gold must be heated seven times to be the purest. Could be. God uses the number "seven" often to denote perfectness—or the whole.

Learning to be a disciple burns away selfishness. It teaches us to be more understanding with each other, friendlier, unafraid, and gives us the ability to identify with the "least of them." In other words, it teaches us to be foot washers!

"When God wants to drill a man, and thrill a man, and skill a man, when God wants to mold a man to play the noblest part when He yearns with all His heart to produce so great and bold a man that all the world will be amazed, watch His methods, watch His ways. How He hammers him and hurts him, and with mighty blows converts him into trial shapes of clay that only God understands, while his tortured heart is crying and he lifts beseeching hands, How He bends but never breaks, when His good He undertakes. How He uses whom He chooses, and with every spirit infuses him, and by every act endures him to try His splendor out. God knows what He's about."

Anon

The Testing Of Your Faith
James 1:3

"Realize that they come to test your faith" (James 1:2).

Talk is cheap—suffering proves the quality of our faith. *We* don't know the strength of our faith until the trials come!

Abraham was called the "father of the faithful" after he offered his son as a sacrifice. His faith said, "He (Isaac) will die, but *I believe God will give him back to me.*" "And Abraham said to his young men, 'Stay here with the donkey, and I and the lad will go yonder; *and we will*

7

worship and return to you' " (Genesis 22:5). In Hebrews 11:17-19, we read, "By faith Abraham, when he was tested, offered up Isaac; and he who had received the promises was offering up his only begotten son; it was he to whom it was said, 'In Isaac your seed shall be called.' He considered that God is able to raise men even from the dead; from which he also received him back as a type."

Someone has said, "God asked for Isaac, but He was really wanting Abraham." In other words, he was really wanting to know how far Abraham's faith would carry him. How could there be any more important test than for Abraham to give his son of promise?

Many new Christians are so sure of their faith that they make all kinds of rash assurances—only to find that their faith is a weak faith. God mentions many kinds of faith—strong, weak, vain, and dead.

We are reminded of the vain faith of many of the Jewish leaders. "Yet at the same time many even among the leaders believed in Him. But because of the Pharisees they would not confess their faith for fear they would be put out of the synagogue; for they loved the praise from men more than praise from God" (John 12:42-43) NIV

The Quality Of Endurance
James 1:4

"But let the process go on until that endurance is fully developed."

The testing of our faith *gradually* develops in us the ability to endure *whatever, whenever.* Our fears lessen; our strengths increase, and we learn that we can bear the new test or situation. We learn a lot by experience. The sprinter must change to be the confident runner who finishes the marathon. "If we faint in adversity our strength is small" (Proverbs 24:10).

One of the hardest lessons I had to learn as a bride or a young mother was that I could do another task, and another one. No more throwing up my hands and lying down in supposed exhaustion. I found out that I could get up for the two o'clock feeding and the four o'clock feeding, etc. God's tests produce the same information—*you can get up again!* Someone wisely observed, "The mark of a true Christian is getting up one more time than you fall."

Mature With Integrity And No Weak Spots
James 1:4

Isn't that what we want, most of all? A mature character—women of integrity with *no weak spots?* The acquiring of endurance produces all this. Perseverance, and patience, sometimes hanging on by our teeth have their results of no weak spots. Integrity means we become trustworthy. Maturity means we have grown up and put away childish things. No weak spots mean we are no longer vulnerable.

Is Every Answer In The Book?
James 1:5

Every *principle* for answers and examples is in the Book—but not every personal answer for your particular problem. So, what do we do? The answers are still in this same section of scripture. "And if, in the process, any of you does not know how to meet any particular problem he has only to ask God—who gives generously to all men without making them feel foolish or guilty—and he may be quite sure that the necessary wisdom will be given him."

We should pray daily—sometimes hourly—for His wisdom. Faith tells us we will get it! But, we must pray in faith, knowing that He cares, that He is involved in our every decision and that He will answer that request according to His will.

If we don't believe that, don't bother to pray. "But he must ask in sincere faith without secret doubts as to whether he really wants God's help or not. A man of divided loyalty will reveal real instability at every turn" (James 1:6-8).

In Conclusion

'I'd rather be ashes than dust. I would rather have my spark burn out in a brilliant blaze than be stifled by dry rot. I would rather be a superb meteor, every atom of me in magnificent glow, than a sleepy and perseverant planet. The proper function of a man is to live, not to exist."

Jack London

And we could say, "The proper function of a Christian is to suffer whatever is required of him."

A Prayer To Grow

I've never grown to where I say,
"Lord, send more pain and hurt my way."
Instead, I tend to run away, to cry and pray.
To run and hide and hurt inside.
But each time when I turn and fight
And the battle's won, and things end right.
I glorify His name, I glorify His name.

Lea Fowler

QUESTIONS FOR DISCUSSION

1. How do you know the difference between a trial and a temptation?

2. Why do some families persecute their offspring or relatives for becoming Christians?

3. Name some benefits caused by the suffering process.

A MINISTRY IS GIVEN
Chapter 3 √

Blessed be the God and Father of our Lord Jesus Christ, the Father of mercies and God of all comfort; who comforts us in all our affliction so that we may be able to comfort those who are in any affliction with the comfort with which we ourselves are comforted by God. For just as the sufferings of Christ are ours in abundance, so also our comfort is abundant through Christ. But if we are afflicted, it is for your comfort and salvation; or if we are comforted, it is for your comfort, which is effective in the patient enduring of the same sufferings which we also suffer; and our hope for you is firmly grounded, knowing that as you are sharers of our sufferings, so also you are sharers of our comfort.

2 Corinthians 1:3-7

A young preacher's wife who had lost a child once asked me if I thought God has taken her child to punish her. I replied, "Read 2 Corinthians 1:3-7 and you will find your answer. God put a ministry upon you to make this tragic accident work together for your good and for the good of others."

God set this world spinning and started the forces of nature. A ball thrown up comes back down. An adult leaping off a high building is killed. A small child falling off the same building is killed, too. (God didn't push either of them.)

Accidents happen and will continue to occur as long as there is life and death. But God requires of Christians who have survived such tragedies to wrap up their own loss, in time, and reach out to others who are experiencing that same grief. Hopefully, they, too, will continue the chain of sympathy and understanding.

Let's Study The Text

"Blessed be the God who comforts." Hagar said, "God sees." He sees it all. Nothing escapes His eyes. Especially does He see His family

11

when they are in trouble.

As the old song says, "He promised never to leave me, never to leave me alone." I don't know how non-Christians find the strength to bear their burdens alone!! How do people get along, exist, without the constant care from the Father and His family on earth?

God's family is instructed to rejoice with the rejoicing and to cry with the weepers. The tighter the bond, the more unified the body of Christ, the deeper the love, the more we share of "heaven on earth,": This is God's desire for His own.

This reading tells us that God gives us *all* comfort. His plan is for us to be rocked and held and told that we will get better. God compares Himself to a mother in Isaiah 66:12. "For thus says the Lord, 'Behold, I extend peace to her like a river, and the glory of the nations like an overflowing stream; and you shall be nursed, you shall be carried on the hip and fondled on the knees. As one whom his mother comforts, so I will comfort you.' "

We also read in Isaiah 49:15,16: "Can a woman forget her nursing child, and have no compassion on the son of her womb? Even these may forget, but I will not forget you. Behold, I have inscribed you on the palms of my hands."

What comfort to know He looks on us as His little children who don't know their right hand from their left!

The world, even the church, may not know of a calamity that has just come upon us, but God is there *at the scene!*

In All Afflictions

When we are hurting, He hurts, too. He hastily calls His helpers to ease our minds and bodies. He blesses the skill of the surgeons' hands. He fortifies the prescriptions given. He often reverses the expected outcome. Why pray if there is no hope? And if the particular occasion ends in a death, He picks up the pieces and rebuilds the souls of the ones left.

Why Does He Comfort Us?

There are at least two reasons that He comforts. First, He comforts us for our own benefit. "Thou, who has shown me many troubles and distresses, wilt revive me again, and will bring me up again from the depths of the earth. Mayest thou increase my greatness, and turn to comfort me" (Psalm 71:20,21).

My faith must grow to where it sustains me through whatever evil the day brings. Are you familiar with the saying—"Lord, help me to know that nothing will happen today that you and I together cannot handle."? And the Lord cautions us that each day will have its evil.

Read Hebrews 12:8. Think about it. I believe that it says that only God's illegitimate children are without discipline—or without comfort! In other words, non-Christians do not experience God's chastenings or His comforts.

The second reason He comforts us is so that we will comfort, reassure, bind up, strengthen others who are now suffering acutely. How do we do this? We go to them and say, "Let me tell you, God cares and He will deliver you just like He delivered me!"

Isn't it interesting that the word "comfort" occurs 10 times in this reading! (2 Corinthians 1:3-7)

Why do we suffer in the first place? *The lessons we learn as we heal are only learned through suffering!* Some may truthfully say or feel, "I don't want to suffer so I can help others!" That is an honest reaction. But, it does not please God, for it is a selfish reply. "By suffering we get a chance to partially repay the debt we owe." Anon.

Only a masochist *loves* to suffer. That person needs help. To love pain is sick. But, God wants us to love our neighbor as much as we love ourselves. *We want help* when our world is upside down, and we are in pain. *Pain gets our attention.* If we have hurt enough, we may find sympathy within our hearts to bind another's wounds. God wants us to become veterans, not to remain soldiers in basic training.

The Comfort Of Christ

We Christians are to become ever conscious that we are at war with Satan. Satan, who is the Prince of the Air and Prince of the Earth. We live in his territory. We are in the world but not of it.

Pilgrims, we are. "This world is not my home, I'm just a passing through," one song says. And another, "And the toils of the road will seem nothing when I get to the end of the way."

Christ continues daily to sustain us. He is our life-line to the Father. And God's will is that as we are comforted and protected, we will reach out to our comrades who are in the cross-fire or near a land mine. We are told to "save ourselves" (Acts 2:40). And the paradox of it all is by saving others, *we save ourselves.*

Paul's Plea

The apostles recognized that every time they were afflicted, there were benefits. Their feelings were: If we are jailed, we are strengthened to bear your trials; if we are beaten, we can sing and get up and preach again, and if we die, we are released to a better world. If we are freed from any particular trial, this should give us heart. When you see us bear with patience our chains, this should give you the. example of bearing your own chains.

13

We are promised in 2 Timothy that any who would live a godly life will suffer persecution. *Those who would be the greatest in the kingdom, the foot washers, will have to suffer more than others.* "And indeed all who desire to live godly in Christ Jesus will be persecuted" (2 Timothy 3:12).

But, are we mindful of the preceding verses which show how the apostles' experiences help us to be cross bearers? "But you followed my teaching, conduct, purpose, faith, patience, love, perseverance, persecutions, sufferings. . . . .what persecutions I endured, and out of them all the Lord delivered me" (2 Timothy 3:10,11).

What would we do today without the examples of fellow Christians who have suffered and survived? When you have lost a child, who do you hope will come? One who has lost a child. When you have lost your mate? A faithful widow. When you are bankrupt? One whose finances have finally worked out after disaster. When you have fallen away? One who understands temptation.

And so Paul closes this teaching with this thought. "And our hope for you is steadfast; knowing that, as ye are partakers of the sufferings, so also are ye of the comfort." We must be interns, those called in emergencies, trained by our own fearful experiences to administer God's given oxygen of hope and healing.

I can show the lonely, broken hearted
I can show the low income person that God blesses them with health, children too

I can show young its not easy to give up God, like the bad relationships

I can show the ones with disabilities they can be useful + serve in God's kingdom He will use you too

THE COMFORT OF GOD

In times of grief and pain we say,
"We'll never laugh again—no way."
But, we will!
Our hearts beat fast as we shrink in fright—
Yet time will bring "songs in the night."
Troubles will only make us grow.
They often come to make us know
That Satan can never bring any woe
That is stronger than the comfort of God.

Lea Fowler

I can show that God can save you from physical death

I can show the shy / untalented ones, they can teach / serve

those who have high education can do great things they can help others. He'll use you too

QUESTIONS FOR DISCUSSION

1. What ministry do you have to offer?
I can show that one can be tough + serve even when in physical pain

2. Are you suffering persecutions for His name? *yes*
If not, why not?

3. Tell of an occasion where you "bound up a wound."

I can show the one who deal with loved ones who are alcoholics / suicide, that they can keep going
I can show women how to be happy with God

REMEMBER JOB
Chapter 4

For patience *as you suffer,* God says to remember Job. Job was a better person than we are, or than most of us. In fact, he was the best man living at that time. He was called "perfect" (in good working order), and he proved it by his endurance while suffering.

In that day and it is still thought true, that if you suffer, you have sinned and if you are blessed (especially financially), you are all right with God. We are in danger when we think that every material blessing is a sign that we are well pleasing in God's sight! When things go wrong financially, do we feel that we have lost God's favor? Do we feel that we are being punished and are out of God's favor? Or if our finances continue to increase, is that a positive proof we are in "the narrow way?" REMEMBER SATAN OFFERED JESUS THE WEALTH OF THE WORLD FOR A PRICE!

So, God inspired a book to teach us good people have it bad—sometimes, in spite of their godly lives. Don't remember just Job's sores, but do remember the end of the matter was God's compassion for Job. And we are to remember today how our particular ordeals end as God's compassion works in our lives.

The First Test

God set up the test. He said to Satan, "Have you considered my servant Job? There is no one on earth like him; he is blameless and upright, a man who fears God and shuns evil" (Job 1:8). NIV

Satan answers, "Does Job fear God for nothing? Have you not put a hedge around him and his household and everything he has? You have blessed the work of his hands, so that his flocks and herds are spread throughout the land. But stretch out your hand and strike everything he has, and he will surely curse you to your face" (Job 1:9-11). NIV

Let's consider the challenge. God has thrown down the gauntlet. God is saying, in essence, that Satan has failed to defeat Job's godly life. *God knew the outcome of what Satan could do and what Job would*

15

do. (It has always been a principle of God's to see that His obedient children will never be tempted above what they are able to bear. What a comfort!)

Satan undoubtedly knew about Job's good life and his God-given blessings. But, Satan, the Accuser, gives a bad motive for Job's faithfulness.

Satan says that Job is just being good for what he can get! That God has him guarded and safe within a fence. (We, too can be in a fence with our Shepherd, watching for our souls.)

"Let me take away his material and physical blessings, and he'll quit you. He's only in it for what he can get! Listen to him curse you when you take away his blessings."

God answered, "Everything he has is in your hands, but on the man himself do not lay a finger" (Job 1:12). NIV (Remember God always restricts Satan when Satan is dealing with His faithful children!)

So, Satan takes all of Job's oxen and sheep and camels—one herd right after the other. (Have you noticed how many times Satan kicks you when you are down?) Evidently Job was able to bear these tests well. Then, he brings the worst heartbreak of all. Satan causes all of Job's ten children to die at one time! (Mankind tends to blame *God* for every tornado, car wreck, sickness, and death.) *This was Satan's work—not God's!* "The last *enemy* to be destroyed is death" (1 Corinthians 15:26).

Jesus defeated the power of death when He was raised from the dead. He "bound the strong man" and freed the Christians to live eternally.

". . .that through death, he might render powerless him who had the power of death, that is, the devil; and might deliver those who through fear of death were subject to slavery all their lives" (Hebrews 2:14-15).

Satan is always hoping to be permitted to hurt a Christian. How gratified he must have been to give the apostle Paul a "messenger of Satan," a thorn. "There was given to me a thorn in my flesh, a messenger of Satan, to torment me. Three times I pleaded with the Lord to take it away from me. But he said to me, 'My grace is sufficient for you, for my power is made perfect in weakness" (2 Corinthians 12:7-9).

We know Job took all of these tests as we hope we would in like circumstances. "Naked I came from my mother's womb, and naked I shall return there. The Lord gave and the Lord has taken away, blessed be the name of the Lord. Through all this Job did not sin nor did he blame God" (Job 1:21-22).

The Second Test

Again God challenged Satan with the same words, "Have you considered my servant Job?" Satan offers another dare: Let me hurt his body. "Skin for skin, yes, and all that a man has he will give for his life" (Job 2:4).

God answered again, "Don't kill him." And Satan went to work, no doubt joyfully and probably over-confidently.

Skin For Skin

Could we endure unbearable, constant pain? We'll never know until we are tested to that degree. How long could *we* endure torture? Not long, I fear. Satan said, "A man will give all he has for his own life.. But stretch out your hand and strike his flesh and bones, and he will surely curse you to your face" (Job 2:4-5).

Many people *do* curse God when they suffer. They raise fists of rage, and some even die cursing God—who probably did not cause the ordeal. What a way to face God in the last moments!

Immediately Satan "afflicted Job with painful sores from the soles of his feet to the top of his head" (Job 2:7). Some translations say that the sores were boils.

(People of today do not seem to have boils as they used to. I remember during the Depression many had them. It could have been caused by what we ate or didn't eat. Boils are very painful and sometimes have to be lanced by a doctor.)

Job Sat Among The Ashes

Remember Satan's aim was to have Job curse God. "Thus artfully is the temptation managed with all the subtlety of the old serpent, who is here playing the same game against Job that he played against our first parents, aiming to seduce him from his allegiance to his God and to rob him of his integrity." Matthew Henry

Job sat and scraped his sores with no one to help him. A former wealthy man who was accustomed to servants suffered alone. Most of his servants, and all of his children were dead. He continually scraped the boils, for they were a long time healing.

"He has not wherewithal to fee a physician or surgeon, and, which is most sad of all, none of those he has formally been kind to had so much sense of honor and gratitude as to minister to him in his distress, and lend him a hand to dress or wipe his running sores, either because the disease was loathsome and noisome or because they apprehended it to be infectious."

Matthew Henry

He raked his sores continually day and night. At night he wished for daytime, and in the day he longed for night.

Why did he sit in the ashes? I really don't know for sure. I know it was the custom under the Old Law for the Jews to throw ashes on their heads in times of despair. It probably was a sign of humility and a plea for God's mercy.

The Wife's Lament

His wife urged him to "curse God and die." He answered by calling her a "foolish woman," *not an evil woman.* Remember she, too, had lost all of her children and now she sees Job, who was once the richest and most respected man of their day, sitting and suffering in the ash heap.

Job's Wife

Dost thou not see that thy devotion's vain?
What have thy prayers procured but woe and pain?
Hast thou not yet thy int'rest understood?
Perversely righteous, and absurdly good?
Those painful sores, and all thy losses, show
How heaven regards the foolish saint below.
Incorrigibly pious! Can't thy God
Reform thy stupid virtue with His rod?

Sir R. Blackmore
—quoted by Matthew Henry

Somehow I can't condemn her like this. God did keep her alive, and she bore Job ten more children. I am content to say as Job, "Don't be a foolish woman. Shall we accept good from God, and not trouble?" (Job 2:10)

Surely, Satan used her to tempt Job, but she was at an all time low in her life, too.

The Visiting Tormentors

Job, in time, called the three "miserable comforters." They meant well; they were old friends and religious men. When they saw Job, they did not recognize him. Their old friend looked more like a leper than a wealthy "prince." For seven days and seven nights, they sat on the ground with Job, speechless because of his pain.

Did God or Satan send them? Surely Job was thrilled to see them. But, as they sat those seven days, it seemed as if they weighed Job and found him wanting.

It is true that Job spoke first and bewailed his birth, his sufferings, and even God's part in the whole matter. But, they answered with no consolation or understanding. Their words went from bad to worse. The three of them told Job over and over, "You are a guilty man and you are just covering your sins." *They said so much that they shouldn't have said.* In fact, at the end of the book of Job it is recorded that God not only scolded *them* but also commanded Job to make sacrifices for the forgiveness of *their* sins.

Eliphaz

Eliphaz, the oldest, said, "If you return to the Almighty, you will be restored; if you remove unrighteousness from your tent" (22:23). He also said, "Is not your wickedness great, and your iniquities without end? For you have taken pledges of your brothers without cause, and stripped men naked. To the weary you have given no water to drink, and from the hungry you have withheld bread" (22:5-7). These were all untrue charges, for Job had been a very merciful and generous man.

At one time, Job says to the three, "Pity me, pity me, O my friends, for the hand of God has struck me. Why do you persecute me as God does, and are not satisfied with my flesh?" (19:21-22) In other words, "Doesn't my physical suffering touch your heart? Isn't it bad enough to keep you from railing at me?" This is so sad.

Bildad

Bildad said the cruelest thing of all. "Does God pervert justice or does the Almighty pervert what is right? If your sons sinned against him, then he delivered them into the power of their transgression" (8:3-4). The NIV says it this way, "When your children sinned against him, he gave them over to the penalty of their sin."

They intimated, "Your ten children were violently destroyed because of their sins!" How could Job ever forgive such an accusation? Later, Job penned these moving words, "Oh, that I were as in months gone by, as in the days when God watched over me; when his lamp shone above my head, and by his light I walked through the darkness; as I was in the prime of my days, when the friendship of God was over my tent, when the Almighty was yet with me; and my children were around me; when my steps were bathed with butter" (29:2-5).

Zophar

Zophar accuses Job of being a liar. "For you have said, 'My teaching is pure and I am innocent in your eyes.' But would that God might speak, and open his lips against you" (11:4-5).

Job answered, "Truly then you are the people, and with you wisdom will die! . . . . . .I am a joke to my friends. The one who called on God, and he answered him; the just and blameless man is a joke" (12:2,4).

Did Job Lose His Integrity?

No, he did not. Though he did complain a lot. (Wouldn't you?) *God did not count this complaining as sin.* Though He did reprove Job later for his griping.

Did Job curse God for his suffering? No, he believed he would still live with God in time. "Though he slay me, I will hope in him" (13:15). "And as for me, I know that my Redeemer lives, and at the last, he will take his stand on the earth. Even after my skin is flayed, yet without my flesh I shall see God" (19:25-26).

God Answers Job

When God reproved Job, He said, "Will the fault-finder contend with the Almighty? Let him who reproves God answer it" (40:1-2).

Then Job answered the Lord and said, "Behold, I am insignificant; what can I reply to Thee? I lay my hands on my mouth. Once I have spoken, and I will not answer; even twice, and I will add no more" (40:3-5).

Job realized that he had said too much. But God understood and had compassion. After all, God knows "man is but dust."

"Just as a father has compassion on his children, so the Lord has compassion on those who fear him. For he himself knows our frame; he is mindful we are but dust" (Psalm 103:13-14).

What a comfort to us in all our sufferings, and sins, and bewilderments! *He is there; He cares; He monitors the tests and the temptations.* He keeps accurate books, and there will be a recompense for every victory and mercy for every confessed defeat.

The End Of The Account

God won, Satan lost. The whole story was written down for our learning. We need to read and reread this touching book. Job needs to become our friend and example. In a way, God says to us, "Have *you* considered my servant Job?" "Behold, we count those blessed who endured, you have heard of the endurance of Job and have seen the outcome of the Lord's dealings, that the Lord is full of compassion and is merciful" (James 5:11).

God doubled all of Job's material possessions that he had lost. His wife bore him ten more children. His body was healed, and his respect was restored. His character stood all the tests. (No doubt, he had no trouble bearing the tests and trials of future years.)

Being women, we enjoy the description of his new family. "And in all the land no women were found to be so fair as Job's daughters; and their father gave them inheritance among their brothers!"

"And after this, Job lived 140 years, and saw his sons, and his grandsons, four generations. And Job died, an old man and full of days" (42:15-17).

In Conclusion

Someone may hastily say, "It wasn't fair—what happened to Job!" (Should the clay so question the potter?)

"He wasn't warned, and it wasn't explained to him that God was allowing it, or that he would win or that Satan was the real enemy. And that all of his possessions would be doubled, etc." (We aren't warned either when it is "test day.")

But, remember we have many advantages that Job did not have: the knowledge of Satan and of heaven and hell. We have the complete Bible. He probably had no words of God to read. We have the gift of the Holy Spirit and the examples of the sufferings of Christ and the history of many martyrs.

The bottom line is to remember the *end* of the Lord when you think of Job Remember it all ended right! Remember that patience and endurance paid off for Job—and will for us. *Don't just remember the boils!*

Let's Fly

"I can't take anymore,
I give up," I say.
And He says, "Yes, you can.
I'm here—all the way."
"You don't know how much it hurts,"
*   I cry.*
"My son told me, and I watched Him die."
"Well, heaven better be worth it," I sigh.
"It is, it is, now let go and FLY!"

Lea Fowler

QUESTIONS FOR DISCUSSION

The Bible, The Holy Spirit, history of many martyrs

1. Do you think Job knew there was a Satan?
   No He didn't have our advantage of the Jesus!
2. Do we really know there is a Satan?
   Yes!
3. Why should we not fear sufferings and death itself?
   This life is just a shot while our real home awaits in heaven - no pain.

21

DESERVED CHASTENINGS
Chapter 5

We know by other scriptures that we all fall short (miss the mark) by many constant commissions and omissions in the sin department.

The Punishment Of Sin

One of the most important teachings in the Bible and one we need to stress as we raise our children is, "You'll pay!" God is not fooled—and He keeps "a writing all the time," as an old gospel song teaches us. As they say in the Northeast, "You don't get away with "nawthin."

God picks the time and the place and the appropriate recompense for His vengeance. He reminds us that vengeance belongs to Him. "Vengeance is mine, and retribution, in due time their foot will slip; for the day of their calamity is near, and the impending things are hastening upon them" (Deuteronomy 32:35).

> O Lord, God of vengeance;
> God of vengeance, shine forth!
> Rise up, O Judge of the earth;
> Render recompense to the proud.
> How long shall the wicked, O Lord,
> How long shall the wicked exult?
> They pour forth words, they speak arrogantly;
> All who do wickedness vaunt themselves.
> They crush Thy people, O Lord,
> And afflict Thy heritage.
> They slay the widow and the stranger,
> And murder the orphans.
> And they have said, "The Lord does not see,
> Nor does the God of Jacob pay heed."
> Pay heed, you senseless among the people;
> And when will you understand, stupid ones?
> He who planted the ear, does he not hear?
> He who formed the eye, does he not see?

He who chastens the nations, will he not rebuke,
Even he who teaches man knowledge?
The Lord knows the thoughts of man. . . .

Psalm 94:1-11

And, we are all familiar with the passage in Hebrews 10:30: "For we know him who said, 'VENGEANCE IS MINE, I WILL REPAY," and again, 'THE LORD WILL JUDGE HIS PEOPLE.' "

So, we see His promise to handle His people, His children. Brother Keeble once said, "God doesn't give man the right to avenge, for He knows we would either be too harsh or too lenient."

Our past sins and indiscretions should have taught us by now that SIN DOES NOT PAY! It is too expensive to be in God's disfavor.

Examples Of God's Punishment Fitting The Crime

Do you remember proud Haman who was so angry with Mordecai who would not bow to him? So, he cleverly devised a scheme where not only Mordecai would die but also his whole nation would die violently.

Haman ordered gallows to be built for his enemy, Mordecai, but Haman, himself, was hung on it. Read the book of Esther—it's a treasure.

"He who leads the upright astray in an evil way will himself fall into his own pit" (Proverbs 28:10).

Handsome Absalom, the son of David, was known for his beautiful hair. He had it cut and weighed once a year. He sat at the gates, this fancy politician, and said something like this to the people coming into the city, "If I were judge, everybody's needs would be met. He would get justice from me" (2 Samuel 15:1-5). He would also kiss every person who bowed to him in homage.

Absalom went to war against his broken-hearted father. David commanded his soldiers to spare his son, if they found him. But, that beautiful hair was caught up in the trees, and he was slain.

There are countless examples of God's fitting the punishment to the crime. Don't we see Him doing this often in our own lives?

The Discipline Of Tribulation

"Strengthening the souls of the disciples, encouraging them to continue in the faith, and saying, 'Through many tribulations we must enter into the kingdom of God' " (Acts 14:22).

Jesus warned us that the world would hate us as it hated Him. (Enough to kill him.) He also warned us that often our own families would turn from us when we take on the name of Christ.

23

(It is interesting that we can change political parties, or drop our lodge membership, or wear the name of a man religiously and not suffer such rejection.)

But, God makes these trials strengthen us and teach us endurance.

Exult In Our Troubles

In fact, we are told to exult in our tribulations. "And not only this, but we also exult in our tribulations, knowing that tribulation brings about perseverance; and perseverance proven character, and proven character, hope; and hope does not disappoint, because the love of God has been poured out within our hearts through the Holy Spirit who was given to us" (Romans 5:3-6).

We are to be joyful, even excited, about our tribulations even God's discipline. We know that God loves us because He continues to teach us, train us, and hopefully even change us. If we were not children of God, He would not bother.

"Take away my capacity for pain and you rob me of the possibility for joy. Take away my ability for failure and I would not know the meaning of success. Let me be immune to rejection and heartbreak and I could not know the glory of living." Ross W. Mans

Aren't we relieved that His anger is temporary *if we repent?* Jeremiah 23:20 says, "The anger of the Lord will not turn back until he has performed and carried out the purposes of his heart; in the last days you will clearly understand it." Look at Psalm 103:8-10: "The Lord is compassionate and gracious, slow to anger and abounding in lovingkindness. He will not always strive with us; nor will He keep His anger forever. He has not dealt with us according to our sins, nor rewarding us according to our iniquities."

Perseverance Or Patience

Troubles do work out in time. *Whatever it is will usually pass.* We learn this through experiencing discomfort. Whatever you are suffering right now will not be troubling you a year or so from now. (It may be something worse!)

But, when that something worse is upon us, we can learn to hang on. It has been proven to us by our past victories or even our defeats.

Character Proved

In fact, our patience produces—yes, proves what we are made of. Or we might say what we have become through God's discipline.

What kind of soil are we—shallow or deep? We don't know until after the many difficulties, heartbreaks, and chastenings.

"You can't have "fruitage" until you first have "rootage." Anon.

24

When Peter denied Christ three times, how he must have despised his weakness. WHAT LUXURIES COULD HAVE BEEN OFFERED TO HIM THAT WOULD HAVE MADE HIM FORGET HIS BETRAYAL? None. God allowed Peter to tell us that we "cease from sin when we suffer" (1 Peter 4:1). Peter's character developed to such an extent that he would and did die for the Lord.

"The church offers no easy way, nor can it do so. It is an institution of martyrs and heroes. Most of the men who wrote the New Testament, or dared to follow Christ in the first century, finally wore the martyr's crown. When we as Christians try to live a life of ease, without sacrifice for the cause, we are attempting to unite incompatibles."

Henry Trumble

Which brings us back to the subject that it is through the sufferings that victorious Christians bear that produces the kind of people you "can throw to the lions."

Hope

Hope is the motive for "hanging in there" no matter what. The hope of eternal life is the "one hope" we have. Burton Coffman says, "Paradise lost can yet be paradise regained!"

We should hope to hear the trumpet blow—today. To see our Savior in the clouds, coming after us to take us home. To see our Father who is waiting to greet us, the angels, and heaven itself. We yearn to see no more sufferings and no more temptations from our enemy, the accuser.

The Power Of Our Weaknesses

Paul prayed three times fervently for his thorn of the flesh to be removed, but God refused to remove it. God realized the worth of the thorn. "And because of the surpassing greatness of the revelations, for this reason, to keep me from exalting myself, there was given me a thorn in the flesh, a messenger of Satan to buffet me—to keep me from exalting myself!" (2 Corinthians 12:7)

The thorn took away conceit, and it perfected Paul's needs. God loves paradoxes! This is one of His greatest. Weakness, and only weakness, gets ourselves out of the way. It makes us more useful in His work. It forces us to the Word, looking for answers. Weakness shows us our dependence on the Source. It proves again that even the strongest Christian is not spared troubles, and it reminds us that God is near to the broken spirit. "The Lord is near to the broken hearted, and saves those who are crushed in spirit" (Psalm 34:18). "The sacrifices of God are a broken spirit; a broken and a contrite heart, O God, thou wilt not despise" (Psalm 51:17).

In Conclusion

So, we learn through trial and error that we cannot practice in or continue in sin. "No one who is born of God practices sin because his seed abides in him; and he cannot sin because he is born of God" (1 John 3:9).

He knows he cannot "afford" to sin—it doesn't pay. Its price is far too dear. Suffering burns out the desire for the "no—no's."

It is true we all err, but we should hate the sin and not practice *it*. We *should* be uncomfortable in sin. We *have* to fix it, our part of it, for we cannot live with it. In counting the cost of sin, we *refuse* to indulge in it. We turn from sin to sanity—we cease from sinning.

The Fun Machines

Satan runs the "fun-machines."
Shows us things that should not be seen.
He lusts for all our leisure time
And always hopes to get the prime.
So, he offers us a constant diet of
"Aw, come on, and at least try it."
And always hopes we'll make a steady
Diet of SIN.

Lea Fowler

QUESTIONS FOR DISCUSSION

1. Are you conscious of God's chastenings for your sins?

2. When do you find the most peace of mind? *When in prayer worshiping, when reading God's word.*

3. Do you have a problem loving a brother who is living in sin? *Yes I have a problem letting God & letting God handle them. I hang onto & feel discouraged when I need to let go & let God. Be strong (tough love) when we know people (christians) darkest sins. But we have to remember God loves us with our sins & even though we see degrees of need to work on sins God don't. God say sin is sin*

26

THOUGH FORGIVEN
Chapter 6

*"How blessed is he whose transgressions, whose sin is covered!
How blessed is the man to whom the Lord does not impute iniquity, and in whose spirit there is no deceit."*

Psalm 32:3-5

Several years ago a psychiatrist spoke to an assembly of gospel preachers. He made the observation that over 80% of the patients in mental institutions are there because of guilt!

Sad, to say, many of these patients are Christians! THIS SHOULD NOT BE! The above scripture tells us sin can be covered. Iniquity can be forgiven. Man can—through God's help—live a holy life.

We Are All Sinners, Forgiven Or Unforgiven

"For all have sinned and fall short of the glory of God" (Romans 3:23).

All who are capable of sin *have* sinned. This is why Christ came into the world, to suffer in our place, for the "wages of sin is death." And, we deserve to die.

"Each of us has turned to his own way; But the Lord has caused the iniquity of us all to fall on him" (Isaiah 53:6).

We look around us and pronounce people good or bad, saved or unsaved, nice or spiteful—but God tell us what men really are by nature. "Indeed, there is not a righteous man on earth who continually does good and who never sins. . .Behold, I have found only this, that God made men upright, but they have sought out many devices" (Ecclesiastes 7:20, 29).

The Deceit Of Self-Examination

Humans tend to go to one extreme or the other in everything. One group says, "There's no hope for me," and just gives up. The other group, led by pride, says, "It wasn't all *that* bad," and hardens their heart. These people *need* to feel guilty. "We cannot afford spiritual

27

blind spots." (Roy Demonbreum) Both groups could be lost if they continue that logic.

Many of us are not honest with ourselves as we look at our own selves. Deceit is one of Satan's best tools.

"The plans of the heart belong to man, but the answer of the tongue is from the Lord. All the ways of a man are clean in his own sight. But the Lord weighs the motives. Commit your works to the Lord, and your plans will be established."

Proverbs 16:1-3

We tend to "judge ourselves by ourselves." We comfort ourselves by comparing our lives to the criminals who make the headlines every day or we comfort ourselves by comparing our lives to those of weaker Christians. We say to our selves, *"I* pay my debts; *I'm* not cruel to my family; *I* work hard; *I'm* faithful in my church attendance." We have 'I" trouble!

And the Lord gently reminds us that "when we've done all the things which are commanded to say, 'We are unworthy slaves; we have done only that which we ought to have done' " (Luke 17:10). God reminds us to not think more highly of ourselves than we ought to. Though we get depressed when we are "put down," we usually don't stay that way long. The sun rises, and we're self-satisfied again.

Yet the Lord warns us, "Trust in the Lord with all your heart, and do not lean on your own understanding. In all your ways acknowledge him, and he will make your paths straight. Do not be wise in your own eyes; fear the Lord and turn away from evil" (Proverbs 3:5-7).

The Over Burdened

It is just as bad or maybe worse to feel unforgiven. To go to bed heartbroken and then wake to continue the suffering all day for deeds of the past is unbearable and unscriptural. This is NOT the plan of God for His *faithful* children. (If we are not faithful, we *should* feel guilty.)

God deals with us as children, as sheep, not as with hardened criminals. He is a loving Father. He is on our side! He *wants* us to forgive and *for us to forget* what we were forgiven.

He gives us a conscience, it is true, to remind us of our sins! Paul, in his defense before Felix, said, ". . . .that there shall certainly be a resurrection of both the righteous and the wicked. In view of this, I also do my best to maintain always a blameless conscience both before God and men" (Acts 24:13-16).

A dear friend of ours, Lorenza Crosby, once said, "A digested Bible is the best conscience." In Romans 2:15b, we read, "their thoughts alternately accusing or else defending them."

28

Can we be blameless? Yes. Sinless? No. When we sin and then repent, *we are forgiven*—no matter what the sin was! *We will not be blamed for what is erased.* In fact, our pardoned sins are at the bottom of the sea.

"Who is a God like Thee, who pardons iniquity and passes over the rebellious act of the remnant of his possession? He does not retain his anger forever, because he delights in unchanging love. He will again have compassion on us; he will tread our iniquities underfoot. Yes, Thou wilt cast all their sins into the depths of the sea."

Micah 7:18-19

Sin Is Punished

Sin is always forgiven or unforgiven. The unforgiven is always punished in God's time—and He is no respecter of persons. Some murderers on death's row are converted and forgiven *and yet executed.* We need to remember the guilty thief on the cross with Jesus. He confessed his guilt and asked to be remembered when Jesus came into His kingdom. (Jesus took him into Paradise with Him. Both had nail-scarred hands. This is an example of Jesus loving "the least of them" as we are commanded to do.)

"With the kind thou dost show thyself kind; with the blameless thou dost show thyself blameless; with the pure thou dost show thyself pure; and with the crooked thou dost show thyself astute" (Psalm 18:25-26).

God is not fooled or mocked. He knows our heart. He looks at the inside of man while man judges by the outward appearance.

Satan seeks ever to destroy us. What a travesty to live and die forgiven and yet find no constant joy in our present salvation! How few we would influence by our morbid, unhappy lives. And yet, when we think of David and his guilt and repentance, the *answers* to our own shortcomings are revealed.

David, The Man After God's Own Heart

David sinned such grievous sins! Adultery and guile and murder. And the odd thing about it is that he needed to be *told* about his sins before he really saw them through God's eyes.

The prophet Nathan came to him and told him a story—a parable. There was a poor man who had a little pet lamb. He carried the lamb around in his bosom. There was also a rich man who had many lambs—but he took the poor man's lamb and killed it for supper.

David said, "He doesn't deserve to live! He should repay four fold for what he's done," and Nathan said, *"You are the man!"*

29

David made no defense. He acknowledged his guilt and paid—four fold. He was forgiven, but he paid and paid—even after the death of his child by Bathsheba.

Psalm 51 tells us of David's words about his acknowledged sin and the result of his forgiveness. We see him first pleading for God to wash him from his iniquity—"cleanse me from my sin." He confesses his knowledge of his transgressions and that they are ever before him.

He admits that God is whom he has sinned against and deserves whatever punishment God gives. It will be no more than he deserves! David knows God will punish him. And yet, he pleads as we do when he says, "Blot out all my iniquities."

"Don't leave me," is David's plea. "Make me happy again. Restore to me the joy of *your* salvation. None of these sins has brought me peace of mind or happiness." (Oh, that we would count the cost *before* the deeds are done!)

Then, David states, "What can I do to fix it? Burnt offerings?" No, but a "broken spirit; a broken and a contrite heart, O God, thou wilt not despise" (verse 17).

In verse 13 we find something very interesting. David shows us that we won't be much use to God in teaching others until we are joyful, forgiven servants. "Restore to me the joy of thy salvation, and sustain me with a willing spirit. *Then* I will teach transgressors thy ways, and sinners will be converted to thee" (verses 12 and 13).

The Danger Of Staying Guilty

We *can* harden our hearts, still our consciences, and be lost. "When we are guilty of sin, the Spirit sends out signals that something is wrong. When I ignore the signals, I can become calloused." (Roy Demonbreum)

In Hebrews 6 we are taught about people who could not repent. *It doesn't say that God would not forgive* but that man can be where he doesn't want to hear what God has to say—or anyone else.

"For in the case of those who have once been enlightened and have tasted of the heavenly gift and have been made partakers of the Holy Spirit, and have tasted the good word of God and the powers of the age to come, and then have fallen away, it is impossible to renew the again to repentance, since they again crucify to themselves the Son of God, and put him to an open shame."

Hebrews 6:4-6

ISN'T IS SIGNIFICANT THAT IT WAS THE CHILDREN OF GOD WHO CRUCIFIED CHRIST THE FIRST TIME AND ONLY THE CHILDREN OF GOD

WHO CAN CRUCIFY HIM NOW?

You know, these scriptures should warn us of potential, permanent separation from God. We remember how God swore that the disobedient Israelites would never live with Him eternally. (Hebrews 3:8-12) He let them wander in the wilderness until they died. And, Christians should give serious thought about how they receive the Word of God. If we don't *love* God's words, we cannot be saved.

"And with all the deception of wickedness for those who perish, because they did not receive the love of the truth so as to be saved. And for this reason God will send upon them a deluding influence so that they might believe what is false, in order that they all might be judged who did not believe the truth, but took pleasure in wickedness."

2 Thessalonians 2:10-12

We might quickly respond, "I am *not* wicked. I am not adulterous, nor a thief, etc." But God says, "I call wicked those who do not *love* my words."

God wants us to *know Him,* to cast aside our preconceived ideas of Him.

In Conclusion

Becoming a Christian doesn't make us different, but gives us the opportunity to become different. Our sufferings, which are certain, are to be expected. "Beloved, do not be surprised at the fiery ordeal among you, which comes upon you for your testing as though some strange thing were happening to you: but to the degree that you share the sufferings of Christ, keep on rejoicing: so that also at the revelation of his glory, you may rejoice with exultation. If you are reviled for the name of Christ, you are blessed, because the Spirit of glory and of God rests upon you. By no means let any of you suffer as a murderer, or thief, or evildoer, or a troublesome meddler; but if anyone suffers as a Christian, let him not feel ashamed, but in that name let him glorify God" (1 Peter 4:12-16).

We cannot be sinless, but we can be perfect—or in good working order. *We can be blameless, justified, and pardoned.* We can be excited about His coming—looking forward to His appearing. We can be *sanctified* (set apart for His use), and we can be *well-pleasing in His sight. We need not be guilty or joyless.* And, we can truly sing, "It is well with my soul."

31

Undeserved Guilt

There are good hours and bad days.
Times of shame, times of praise.
Watch God toss our sins into the sea,
Don't reach for them; let them be.
We'll repent for bad that has gone by—
And reach for days that too quickly fly—
When our lights are shining bright
And God is glorified by the sight.
And when guilt tries to hurt us once more
We'll push him out—and slam the door!

Lea Fowler

QUESTIONS FOR DISCUSSION

1. Have all responsible people sinned? *Yes*

2. Can we have a blameless conscience? *Yes*
   repent — God forgives

3. How can our not loving the Word of God affect our destiny?

God says we must love His Word
& ~~Hate~~ Hate evil — To enter Kingdom
of heaven —

32

WE LEARN OBEDIENCE
Chapter 7

"Though he were a son—he learned obedience from the things which he suffered" (Hebrews 5:8).

Jesus Christ was and is a part of the Godhead. In fact, everything that has been made was made by Him.

"All things came into being through him; and apart from him nothing came into being that has come into being."

John 1:3

"He was in the world, and the world was made through him, and the world did not know him."

John 1:10

"Yet for us there is but one God, the Father, from whom are all things, and we exist for him; and one Lord, Jesus Christ, through whom are all things, and we exist through him."

1 Corinthians 8:6

"And he is the image of the invisible God, the first-born of all creation. For in him all things were created both in the heavens and on earth, visible, and invisible, whether thrones or dominions or rulers or authorities—all things have been created through him and for him. And he is before all the things, and in him all things hold together."

Colossians 1:15-17

It was determined before the world was made that mankind could be saved by Christ's coming to the earth. That people who would choose His ways and be obedient to Him would be saved eternally. "Just as he chose us in him before the foundation of the world, that we should be holy and blameless before him. In love he predestined us to adoption as sons through Jesus Christ to himself, according to the kind intention of his will. . .in him we have redemption through his

33

blood, the forgiveness of our trespasses, according to the riches of his grace which he lavished upon us" (Ephesians 1:4-8).

God foreknew that man would sin and yet made man anyhow. He could have made us robots, but there is no greater tribute to God than for man, His creation, made in His image, constantly tempted by Satan, to persevere in his allegiance to God.

God loved man enough to devise a plan for him to come back to Him. Jesus agreed to the way of redemption through His blood. He would be the expiation, satisfaction, for God's forgiveness! For God's justice *and mercy*.

So, the Son of God became the man of sorrows and took on flesh. He felt joy and sorrow, pain and delight, acceptance and rejection. Satan tempted Him sorely in every point.

The Intercessor

Today and as long as the world stands, Jesus will be interceding for the children of God before the Father. He can say, "I know how easy it is to be tempted. I know how clever Satan is. I know how weak the spirit of man is and how much stronger his flesh than his spirit that yearns to please you." He said in Matthew 26:41, "Keeping watching and praying, that you may not enter into temptation; the spirit is willing but the flesh is weak." Paul also said in Romans 7:18, "For I know that nothing good dwells in me, that is, in my flesh; for the wishing is present in me, but the doing of the good is not."

We have a Savior who has lived here and experienced what Life has to offer. In fact, He has lived in circumstances that many of us have not had to bear. He had no permanent, earthly home (Matthew 8:20) after He started his three and a half year ministry. He had very little, if any, physical comforts. Somehow, Jesus and the apostles had a purse and helped many who were poorer than themselves. Never do we see Him asking others for their wealth, though He had friends who were wealthy—among whom were Nicodemus, Joseph of Arimathea, and Zaccheus.

The High Priest

The Jewish high priest was supposed to be a man set apart, an example for the Jewish nation. He was to keep the law as perfectly as he could. He was the only person allowed in the Holy Place. He went there once a year, offering sacrifices for the people and for himself.

We are taught how Jesus became our high priest. He was as human as the Jewish high priest, yet without sin.

"For every high priest taken from among men is appointed on behalf of men in things pertaining to God, in order to offer both

gifts and sacrifices for sins; he can deal gently with the ignorant and misguided, since he himself also is beset with weakness; and because of it he is obligated to offer sacrifices for sins, as for the people, so also for himself."

Hebrews 5:1-3

"This hope we have as an anchor of the soul, a hope both sure and steadfast and one which enters within the veil, where Jesus has entered as a forerunner for us, having become a high priest forever according to the order of Melchizedek."

Hebrews 6:19,20

"Now the main point in what has been said is this: we have such a high priest, who has taken his seat at the right hand of the throne of the Majesty in the heavens."

Hebrews 8:1

Though He was divine, He had compassion on the frailties of men, for He had been tempted in every way that they had been. "Therefore, he had to be made like his brethren in all things, that he might become a merciful and faithful high priest in things pertaining to God, to make propitiation for the sins of the people. For since he himself was tempted in that which he has suffered, he is able to come to the aid of those who are tempted" (Hebrews 2:17,18).

I have heard it said He was as human as His mother and as divine as His Father. He was pure enough to not sin but human enough to want to.

Philip's Request

Philip said to Jesus, "Show us the Father and that will be enough" (John 14:8). In other words, "You've seen God and what is He like? What does He want of us? Is our "followship" adequate? What else can we do to please Him?"

Jesus replied, "Have I been so long with you, and yet you have not come to know me, Philip? He who has seen me and has seen the Father; how do you say, 'Show us the Father'?" (John 14:9)

He was saying, "I am just like my father—in words, in actions, in purpose, and in mind. You haven't really been seeing me but you have been seeing the reflection of God in me."

Isn't that what He wants of us? That we grow into the very image of Christ? That our words, actions, ideals, purposes, and our very thoughts be like His? "But the unspiritual man simply cannot accept the matters which the Spirit deals with—they just don't make sense to him, for, after all, you must be spiritual to see spiritual things. The

35

spiritual man, on the other hand, has an insight into the meaning of everything, though his insight may baffle the man of the world. This is because the former is sharing in God's wisdom, and . . . . .incredible as it may sound, we who are spiritual have the very thoughts of Christ!" (1 Corinthians 2:13-16) Phillips Translation

We should be aiming at acting like our Savior in all circumstances. We, too, should be learning obedience in the things that *we must suffer*.

I have heard of a Christian man who was told he had terminal cancer. His first reaction was, "Then I must die like a Christian!" Suffering was waiting ahead, but faith assured him that God would be with him each step of the way. He, too, recognized that he must obey up to death.

Our Obedience

"And having been made perfect, he became to all those who obey him the source of eternal salvation" (Hebrews 5:9).

Because He perfectly obeyed God, He has the right to ask us to follow, even demand, our complete obedience. Mankind naturally is lazy and wants everything free! We want heaven and earth. We may agree to a "token" acceptance of Jesus as an example but not as "Lord." This is too much to ask!

As someone said, "We want to live like the rich man and die like Lazarus." Mankind is basically selfish. *Suffering has its part in making us unselfish*. We come into the Lord as "takers" and through dying to self, in time, *we should become "givers."*

God is the greatest giver, the supreme example of love. All of us are familiar with John 3:16, "For God so loved the world *that he gave* his only begotten son, that whosoever believeth in him should not perish but have everlasting life." KJV

However, are we mindful of the last verse of John 3? "He who believes in the Son has eternal life; but he who does not obey the Son shall not see life; but the wrath of God abides on him." Now that is a disturbing thought! Believing is easy, but obedience to all that is written is hard—and *against nature*.

Many of us would rather not know that obedience is required. We feel "ignorance is bliss." Or that God won't require of us what we don't know. (Wonder who deceives us with *this* philosophy?)

The books will be opened on the last day, and we will be judged by our faithfulness, our attitudes, our knowledge of the Word, and obedience to it—whether we allow ourselves to ever accept these truths or not. "He who rejects me, and does not receive my sayings, has one who judges him; the word I spoke is what will judge him at the last day. . . .and I know that his commandment is eternal life; therefore the things I speak, I speak just as the Father has told me" (John 12:48,50).

The Obedient Suffering
On The Cross

Jesus did not want to die such a death! Who would? Not I. He asked the Father if there could be another way and even as He asked, He remarked that the cross was why He came to earth. His blood would be the only way anyone would or could be saved who had come to the age of responsibility. It would flow back to Adam and Eve and up to the time the trumpet sounds.

Are *we* ready to take suffering we don't want either? He gave us the example of enduring whatever man and Satan would devise for His suffering. WHATEVER! He never became angry or defeated or said, "This is enough! I won't suffer any more, nothing else!" With the spittle of His face and the thorns of His brow, He submitted to the agonizing whipping, mindful that the horror of the cross still lay ahead. He was humiliated—the King jeered by the crowd—the Creator despised by the created. (Would *our* faith survive humiliation?)

Could our present sufferings help us to obey Him in *whatever* He says? Will our love for Him be strong enough to endure to the end? "If you love me, you will keep my commandments" (John 14:15). Do we love Him *that much* yet?

The perfect example has been set, and we must remember that the Father will not allow us to suffer more than we can bear. (1 Corinthians 10:13) *God's army is made up entirely of volunteers.* We must volunteer daily or find ourselves, eventually, a deserter.

Paul gives us an example of obedience of *whatever* was required of him without exception. "Are they servants of Christ? (I speak as if insane.) I more so; in far more labors, in far more imprisonments, beaten times without number, often in danger of death. Five times I received from the Jews thirty nine lashes. Three times I was beaten with rods. Once I was stoned, three times I was shipwrecked, a night and a day I have spent in the deep. I have been on frequent journeys, in dangers from rivers, dangers from robbers, dangers from my countrymen, dangers from the Gentiles, dangers in the city, dangers in the wilderness, dangers on the sea, dangers among false brethren; I have been in labor and hardship, through many sleepless nights, in hunger and thirst, often without food, in cold and exposure. Apart from such external things, there is the daily pressure upon me of concern for all the churches" (2 Corinthians 11:23-28).

In conclusion, "though he were a Son, He learned obedience from the *things* which he suffered." Things—plural—not the cross alone—but by many things that He suffered. His character and integrity triumphed. Our character and integrity, or lack of it, will either triumph or defeat us. We should be comforted that He learned to suffer as a boy, as a teenager, and as a man. The carpenter's son knew how it felt to hit his thumb with a hammer, or cut himself, or dig out splinters. By the age of twelve, it was said of Him, "And he went down with them and came to Nazareth; and he continued in subjection to them; and his mother treasured all these things in her heart. And Jesus kept increasing in wisdom, and stature, and in favor with God and men" (Luke 2:51,52).

He witnessed sibling rivalry. We know that two of His grown brothers recognized Him as God in the flesh after His resurrection. (They were James and Jude.) His little country town asked Him to leave, for they were offended at His power. He was a prophet without honor in His own hometown.

We see ourselves falling short and often as unusable as broken pottery.

But, "God uses broken things. Broken soil to produce a crop, broken clouds to give rain, broken grain to give bread, broken bread to give strength. It is the broken alabaster box that gives forth perfume. It is Peter, weeping bitterly, who returns to greater power than ever." Vance Hanner

"Although he was a Son, he learned obedience from the things which he suffered; and having been made perfect, he became to all those who *obey him* the source of eternal salvation." Hebrews 5:8,9

He Learned Obedience

He obeyed God and that proved His love,
And now He lives with the Father above.
His words are not grievous;
His burden is light.
They bring peace and comfort
Through day and through night.
It's not long 'til we join Him
So no matter the cost,
Keep me close to Jesus
And not lost with the lost.

Lea Fowler

QUESTIONS FOR DISCUSSION

1. Name some things Jesus learned through suffering.

2. How do we know that any temptation will not be too much for us?

3. What is Jesus doing in our behalf now?

God says so
I Cor. 10:13

Because of Jesus
our sins can be
forgiven. We can talk
to our father. He's
preparing a home for us - The ones
who love Him which he can tell
by who obeys His Commandments

→ We can learn through our
suffering not to be selfish
To depend on God like He wants
us to

39

THE AGONY OF
CHURCH TROUBLE
Chapter 8

And agony is what it is! I have witnessed it twice—hopefully that will be all for my lifetime. Once I bore it as a new Christian—the other time as an older Christian.

What Causes All Trouble In The Body Of Christ?

Satan's takeover. Tinsdale's commentary notes, "We waste our time fighting people; we should be fighting Satan—who seeks to control people and make them oppose the work of God."

The Holy Spirit says it this way, "And the Lord's bond servant must not be quarrelsome, but be kind to all, able to teach, patient when wronged, with gladness correcting those who are in opposition, if perhaps God may grant them repentance leading to the knowledge of the truth, and they may come to their senses and escape from the snare of the devil, having been held captive, by him to do his will" (2 Corinthians 2:24-26).

Many young Christian men love the excitement of discord and debate. Aggression has a natural hold on them. "Therefore I want the men in every place to pray, lifting up holy hands, *without wrath and dissension*" (1 Timothy 2:8). Some do not respect the "gray head" nor do they have a desire for God's wisdom. "Do not sharply rebuke an older man, but rather appeal to him as a father" (1 Timothy 5:1), God instructs.

The Kingdom

The concept of a kingdom to a democratic American man (especially a young man) is hard to grasp. Americans vote on *everything*—the majority wins whether it is truth or error. History has proved the majority is usually wrong. It was the crowd who yelled, "Crucify Him, crucify Him!"

Satan attacks our unguarded places for a beachhead. He easily finds many such places in the mission fields where there are few, if any, men yet qualified to serve as elders. (Statistics I've read say it takes twenty to twenty-five years to "home grow" an elder.)

The Catholic church in Rome was set up identically to the Roman government. Many American denominations today are organized as our government—by vote and majority rule. Truth or error can be voted in or out.

But God teaches us that we are under a King. He teaches us rebellion "is as the sin of divination (sorcery) and insubordination is as iniquity and idolatry" (1 Samuel 15:23). GOD DOES NOT PUT UP WITH REBELLION. He handles it—in His time and in His way.

"The Lord knows how to rescue the godly from temptation and to keep the unrighteous under punishment for the day of judgment and especially those who indulge the flesh in its corrupt desires and despise authority. Daring, self-willed. . . . . ." (2 Peter 2:9-10).

The Sin Of Presumption

David said that presumption is a great transgression. Presumption says, "God doesn't care if you change the rules;" (Cain thought that but Abel didn't.) or "Your wisdom surely equals God's, for after all, you are made in His image."

But God answers, "For as the heavens are higher than the earth, so are my ways higher than your ways—and my thoughts than your thoughts" (Isaiah 55:8-9).

No, we must pray as David did, "Also keep back thy servant from presumptuous sins, let them not rule over me. Then I shall be blameless and I shall be acquitted of the great transgression" (Psalm 19:13).

What Is God's Answer
To All The Churches?

Study. Grow up. Let God have His way. Suffering is one way God teaches us maturity. Listen to this article:

STEPS TO MATURITY

Maturity is the ability to handle frustration, control anger, and settle differences without violence or destruction. Maturity is patience. It is the willingness to postpone gratification, to pass up the immediate pleasure or profit in favor of the long term gain. Maturity is perseverance, sweating out a project or a situation in spite of opposition and discouraging setbacks. Maturity is selflessness, responding to the needs of others. Maturity is the capacity to face unpleasantness and disappointment without becoming bitter. Maturity is the gift

41

of remaining calm in the face of chaos. This means peace, not only for ourselves, but for those with whom we live and for those whose lives touch ours. Maturity is the ability to disagree without being disagreeable. Maturity is humility. A mature person is able to say, "I was wrong." He is also able to say, "I am sorry." And when he is proven right, he does not have to say, "I told you so." Maturity is the ability to make a decision, to act on that decision, and to accept full responsibility for the outcome. Maturity means dependability, integrity, keeping one's word. The immature have excuses for everything. They are the chronically tardy, the no-shows, the gutless wonders who fold in the crisis. Their lives are a maze of broken promises, unfinished business and former friends. Maturity is the ability to live in peace with that which we cannot change.

Anonymous

What Causes Trouble Within The Older Churches?

Many times it is the lust for power, the excess of pride, the desire for pre-eminence that causes trouble.

Diotrephes was a prime example of a trouble maker. He wanted the sole rule. The apostle John, as an old man, wrote, "I wrote something to the church, but Diotrephes who loves to be first among them, does not accept what we say. For this reason, if I come, I will call attention to his deeds which he does unjustly accusing us with wicked words; and not satisfied with this, neither does he himself receive the brethren, and he forbids those who desire to do so, and puts them out of the church" (3 John 9-10).

CAN YOU IMAGINE ANY MAN OF GOD NOT ACCEPTING THE WORDS OF THE APOSTLE JOHN? Or putting people out of the church who should be received? (This should give us heart when we see the same thing in the church today. It is not new.)

Too many of us are idealists, and too few are realists. Jesus was a realist—He knew what was in the heart of man and loved him in spite of it.

The church is made up of people in all classifications—babes and mature men and the in between. We have carnal and spiritual, the good fish and the bad (Matthew 13:48-48). There is the sinner and the hypocrite in every body of Christ.

There has ever been and will ever be men like the apostles, and also men like Judas, Stephen the martyr, and Demas who loved something in Thessalonica. And, there will be churches like Philippi and Corinth—the stable and the unstable.

42

Don't let Satan deceive you and fall away because you find the bad tree or the bad fish in the church. The good trees are there, too, and you will know them by their fruits.

I was studying with a lady during the first church trouble, and she was close to becoming a Christian. A neighbor warned her of becoming a part of that troubled group. She asked me if it was true—that we were "at war" and I had to admit it was.

"How will I know which group is right," she asked.

"By their fruits. Stay away from the violent—and close to the peacemakers," I told her. She obeyed the gospel and stayed faithful for the rest of her life.

Matthew Henry, a religious commentator, says, "The worst thing we can bring to a religious controversy is anger."

I heard a wonderful lesson by Dr. John Barton, professor at Northeastern Christian Junior College. The lesson was entitled, "The Quest for Authority." (It works in the world or the church.)

He said that the way of the "Gentile" is:

1. Learn the techniques.

2. Get the man out ahead of you

3. Get what you want—which is the spirit of Diotrephes.

Dr. Barton gave as a Biblical example Herod killing all the little boys to rid himself of Jesus, the future King. He also mentioned Absalom who wanted the kingdom even if it cost the death of his own father, David. Dr. Barton concluded by showing God's way for those who would be great in the kingdom:

1. Ability—Use what talents you have for God's glory.

2. Service—The greatest will be the one who works with no thought of reward and works the hardest at the dirtiest jobs.

3. These two lead to influence and example and appointment to office—if qualified and desired, without seeking it!

Ability applies to those who "take authority." Service applies to those who are "given authority" by the Holy Spirit to be God's leaders.

(Used by permission)

How Do You Survive Strife In The Kingdom??

First, you realize that strife is not unusual. Not only does Jesus walk among the churches, but also Satan, the Accuser, does too. Second, you study. 1 Corinthians 11:18-19 says, "For in the first place, when you come together as a church, I hear that divisions exist among you; and in part, I believe it. For there must be factions among you, in order that those who are approved may have become evident among you."

"In giving you these instructions I must mention a practice which I cannot commend; your meetings tend to do more harm than good. To begin with, I am told that when you meet as a congregation you fall into sharply divided groups, and I believe there is some truth in it for dissensions are necessary if only to show which of you members are sound." New English Bible

You might ask, "How will I know who is sound?"

Watch those who cause divisions. Watch those who yell and argue. Watch those who are vying for a following.

Some wise person said, "When a man wants to draw disciples after him, he must teach another doctrine. A good Christian man will not have his own disciples."

Read Psalms daily. Over and over. Study Psalms in depth; note that God is seeing it all, that HE WILL WIN, that He will avenge, and that the bad won't last forever! Peace will come in time. Listen to Psalm 37:32-36:

The wicked spies upon the righteous,
And seeks to kill him.
The Lord will not leave him in his hand,
Or let him be condemned when he is judged.
Wait for the Lord, and keep his way.
And he will exalt you to inherit the land;
When the wicked are cut off, you will see it.
I have seen a violent, wicked man
Spreading himself like a luxuriant tree in its
native soil.
Then he passed away, and lo, he was no more;
I sought for him, but he could not be found.

Next, you pray, in fact, you beg. And you do it without ceasing.

Name the troublers before the throne daily. You will learn to love them in the process even if they don't repent. You will become sorry for them, as you realize that they are guilty of insubordination to the King, unknowingly. Rather you feel for them—*and you should.*

Is there a cure? You bet. It is time, time, time. Your faith increases as you see Him working, and He is.

Scriptures will come to your mind, such as: "God scatters the people who delight in war;" "Adversity pursues sinners;" "The way of the transgressor is hard;" "This, too, will pass;" "God causes all things to work together for good for those who love Him," and "God will not give you more than you can bear."

You will probably suffer sleeplessness, worry, maybe even a weakening of your faith—but just hold on. REMEMBER THE CHURCH

BELONGS TO JESUS CHRIST AND HE IS NOT A LOSER! The Rock stands, and only those are ground down who assault the Rock.

Can Women Be A Part Of The Trouble?

Oh, yes. I heard a preacher make the remark that he had never seen church trouble that didn't start with a woman. I hope that is not true. What could be a cause for women to be at war? Well, jealousy for a starter. "But, if you have bitter jealousy and selfish ambition in your heart, do not be arrogant and so lie against the truth. This wisdom is not that which comes down from above, but is earthly, natural, demonic. For where jealousy and selfish ambition exist, there is disorder and every evil thing" (James 3:14-16).

Many men desire the lead through pride and selfish ambition, and their wives have the same problem. The wives often contribute to their husbands' overdose of pride.

What can we do to help the jealous person? NOTHING!!!!!

"For jealousy enrages a man and he will not spare in the day of vengeance. He will not accept any ransom, nor will he be content though you give him many gifts" (Proverbs 6:34-45).

A jealous person is on fire—he is looking for a way to wreak vengeance upon the person he (or she) is jealous of. You cannot devise anything that will put out the flame that burns within their hearts. No amount of gifts or kindnesses will ease the situation!

Their only hope for themselves is to keep reading the word, keep praying, keep growing, and God may restore sanity through His loving kindness in time. (Have you ever wondered how many who obeyed the gospel at Pentecost had once said, "Crucify Him, crucify Him!"? And a loving Jesus forgave.)

Note: Both troubled churches have been or are being restored to peace. They are both stronger than they were before the trouble. Men rise and fall, but GOD WILL HAVE THE LAST WORD! God is going to triumph. Will we be a part of His success or a hindrance? Suffering, too, can prepare us for unity.

Search For Peace

To tear up the Body is a terrible sin.
It's to fight a battle that you never can win.
Souls are lost that you cannot restore.
Friendships are broken—homes open no more
To the ones we once held so dear.
Walls are built up that seldom come down,
Satan rejoices as saints lose their crown.

*"Save yourselves," are the words that keep coming to
mind
Though the way to peace is hard to find.*

Lea Fowler

QUESTIONS FOR DISCUSSION

1. Are you a survivor from any church trouble?

2. If so, how did you survive?

3. How can we avoid future church trouble?

WE ARE NEVER ALONE
Chapter 9

Whatever you are suffering is not new to mankind! Thousands are feeling the exact pain you are at the same time. But that doesn't really help *you,* does it?

"Time is the answer," we hear from family, friends, and brethren. Only time. You will not always hurt as you now do. You *will* smile again. That doesn't seem to help much, either!

We want relief *now!* Not twenty years from now. We want the acute pain gone today. *We can't stand anymore.* Where do we go for comfort, for understanding, for sympathy or for problem solving?

If possible, to someone who has survived the same agony. We've already mentioned in another chapter that God gives Christian survivors a ministry. As we reach for them, they should be searching for us. Pray for God to reveal where they are—and let them in when they come.

What Should I Say In The House Of Grief?

Most of us are at a loss when we enter the house of grief or heartbreak. We stumble in our thoughts and words. They usually don't hear our words, but they do remember that we came or wrote or touched. *They remember we cared!*

Should we telephone? This is a hard one. If something tragic has happened to a loved one who lives far away, I, personally, find it hard to make the phone call. Knowing how emotional I am and fearing their emotional state, what if they would *rather not* talk at this particular time? I don't want to add to their grief. In these cases, I usually write a long letter. If this is an incident of local tragedy, of course I go.

What Do We Say Later On?

Let them guide you. Some *want* to talk about their loss or misfortune. Some don't. A friend of mine lost a young nephew. When the family was together, this boy's name was never mentioned—thinking

47

to spare the grieving mother. Years later, she told them how much she had wanted to talk about this son. She *wanted* to remember him! (I've noticed that often some sweet, funny memory seems to help ease the current pain.)

In the "Reader's Digest" a true account was told of a little girl who had lost her little friend who lived next door. On her own, she went and visited the mother of the little girl. When she came back and told her own mother where she had been, her mother asked incredulously, "What did you say?"

She answered, "I crawled up on her lap, and we both cried." Neither child nor grieving mother will ever forget this gesture from the heart of a child.

Never Alone

"He promised never to leave me, never to leave me alone," are the words to an old song. Did He promise that? ". . .for He Himself has said, "I WILL NEVER DESERT YOU, NOR WILL I EVER FORSAKE YOU,' so that we confidently say, 'THE LORD IS MY HELPER, I WILL NOT BE AFRAID. WHAT SHALL MAN DO TO ME?' " (Hebrews 13:5,6)

Christ knows how much you are hurting from whatever pain you are experiencing. Friends may desert you; family may ignore you, and neighbors may forget you, but Jesus never leaves you. *He is never too busy.* He stays as long as you need Him and does not weary with your slow healing.

What If This Pain Is God's Chastening?

He is still there. He monitors what we can bear and what we can't. Discipline is sometimes necessary. "For the commandment is a lamp, and the teaching is light; and reproofs for discipline are the way of life" (Proverbs 6:23). Even chastening is a loving gesture. We often spare the rod with our own child, but God doesn't.

He is fair. He warns. "Do not be deceived, God is not mocked; for whatever a man sows, this he will also reap" (Galatians 6:7). God isn't fooled by anything or anybody. His books are accurate.

We have noted before how effectively God fits the punishment to the crime. Such as: Haman hung on his own gallows; Jacob, the deceiver, deceived by his own father-in-law and the price Lot paid for moving his family toward Sodom. Have you ever noticed what He chooses to "reward us for our iniquities?" Think about it.

How Does He Get Our Attention?

Often through our suffering. Even when we are living a supposedly calm, Christian life, "we need interruptions," says C.S. Lewis. *Apathy does not lead to zeal.* A comfortable rut can be dangerous.

Think how quickly we go back to the way we were after the suffering is over—after the lesson is learned! *God wants us to be saved more than we want to be saved!* Satan loves for us to think ourselves well off spiritually while he knows we are drifting away from the shore. And we don't realize we're drifting.

So, God calls a halt! The rich man loses money or finds he is raising a juvenile deliquent due to the father's own neglect and avarice. The poor man loses sleep or health or friends or you name it. They both hopefully turn back to their Source of strength and their Architect to help rebuild their lives. Sadder and wiser—and holier because they suffered. Because God awakened them.

So, the sufferings come as the needs arise. The quicker we learn, the better! The more we sin, the more we need the Father's attention. The further we drift, the more we need the alarm to sound. The sound of the siren to bring us back to our spiritual lighthouse.

How do we handle God's interruptions? We frantically reach for the lifesaver. "Humble yourselves, therefore, under the mighty hand of God, that he may exalt you at the proper time, casting all your anxiety upon him because he cares for you" (1 Peter 5:6,7). God is saying, "Give your problem to me. I can handle it, but learn from it."

And as we finally slip our mooring to cross Jordan, we are not alone, even then. As the old song goes, "We won't have to cross Jordan alone."

Our Life-Saver

When you climb to the crest and lean over,
He's there, pulling you back.
When you're slipping out of your harness,
He's there, tightening the slack.
When you feel you can't fight any longer,
He gives you just one more deep breath.
He holds out the needed encouragement
When you feel the cold hand of death.
He loves at all times.
Through thick and through thin.
With His protection and wisdom,
You finally win.

Lea Fowler

QUESTIONS FOR DISCUSSION

1. When we are suffering, what do we want the most?

2. How do you respond to the death of a friend?

3. What is God's motive in chastenings?

HE GIVES SONGS IN THE NIGHT
Chapter 10 ✓

It is three o'clock in the morning, and I found I had to get up and share with you what I am beginning to understand about a certain scripture. "He gives you songs in the night" (Job 34:10). That scripture has always bothered me. I had many times deliberately tried to think of songs in the night. I hadn't understood the first part—*He* gives you songs—He, God, gives you songs. It is not—"I strive to sing songs in the night."

This night after I had supposedly recovered from painful arthritis, it struck me again—suddenly. It felt as if my hand, my right hand, was broken. I took Anacin, and my husband consoled me and told me he would be praying as I was for immediate relief. I kept asking myself and God—why, why had this suddenly come back? The timing was bad, I thought. I had the ladies' class coming on Tuesday night, and this was early Sunday morning, the Lord's Day, when I needed to be ready for the most important day of the week.

And then, for the first time I understood the "songs in the night." As I lay there, praying, the songs of joy began to overflow in my heart. Peace settled over me, and I rejoiced at His presence as never before. In the night there is complete quiet time. There are no interruptions. God never sleeps, and when you check in with Him, He is there. What am I saying?

I am saying that suffering is one of God's ways to get our attention. It awakes us, literally and spiritually to just how good we really have it! One of my first concerns was—but I must get back to writing the book and how can I when I am crippled in my writing hand?

But, God was saying, "Trust me, I'm here, and it is more important *what* you write than *when* you write." I had through the years tried to manufacture "songs in the night." I had lain and repeated the words from familiar songs such as, "Count Your Many Blessings," or "Be Not Dismayed What'ere Betide, God Will Take Care of You," but that was ME giving *God* "songs in the night."

Why—In The Night?

There are always distractions in the daytime. As you try to meditate in the day, you are unconsciously aware that the phone may ring, or the dogs may get sick, or some sort of useless emergency may develop. (Satan sees to that!) But, when the household is asleep, you have quality time. And I didn't realize that until this early morning.

"When I remember thee on my bed, I meditate on thee in the night watches, for thou hast been my help, And in the shadows of thy wings I sing for joy. My soul clings to thee, thy right hand upholds me" (Psalm 63:6-8).

What was going on in David's life when he wrote this? Read the following verses. He was suffering. He was afraid for his very life. Many kings and prophets were killed. David himself was later pursued by his own son who sought to kill him and take over the kingdom.

Note the following verses: "But those who seek my life, to destroy it, will go into the depths of the earth. They will be delivered over to the power of the sword, they will be a prey for foxes" (Psalm 63:9,10).

When did all these thoughts come flooding into David's mind—a man after God's own heart? In the night watches, and what made him sing for joy? God is and will be my help. He is mindful of my enemies. He is aware of my fears, and He will vindicate me—so I sing for joy.

I had tried to sing for joy when I was joyful—but we sing for joy when we are scared, or hurting, or weak and have found relief.

Meditation Opens Understanding

"I will meditate on thy precepts, and regard thy ways. I shall delight in thy statutes; I shall not forget thy statutes, I shall not forget thy word" (Psalm 119:15,16). One of the key words in this reading is "delight." Meditation gives delight. Comfort spreads in our being. Verses and thoughts come to mind with new meanings and deeper understandings.

Thoughts like: "There is none like the God of Jeshurum (Israel), who rides the heavens to your help. And through the skies in his majesty. The eternal God is a dwelling place and underneath are the everlasting arms. . .So Israel dwells in security" (Deuteronomy 34:26-28). But, when do I recognize this need? When I need Him the most. When I suffer. When my faith needs to be strengthened and while it is being reinforced. *I know He is there in the night.* The words of the song, "When peace like a river attendeth my way, when sorrow like sea billows roll," then, "It is well with my soul."

I Will Meditate On All Thy Work

"I, will meditate on all thy work, and muse on all thy deeds, thy

52

way, O God, is holy; what god is great like our God? Thou art the God who workest wonders;" (Psalm 77:12,13). His power comes into our minds; His great strength, His omniscience, His omnipotence, His omnipresence. God, with all His power and majesty, cares about *us, personally!*

Why? Our finite minds are astounded at this thought. What is that line in the song—"Sent Him to die, I scarce can take it in"? I pull up to my chin, figuratively, the comfort of this glorious thought. I am beginning to understand why He gives us songs in the night.

Let My Meditation Be Acceptable

"Let the words of my mouth and the meditation of my heart be acceptable in thy sight, O Lord, my rock and my Redeemer" (Psalm 19:14).

Do my sufferings bring comfort or a fleeing from His presence? The answer will determine whether there will be songs in the night or lamentations. Can my faith really believe that this, too, *whatever it is,* will work together for good? Can I believe that these testings and trials are going to strengthen my weak spots, mature my character, and make me a woman of integrity? (James 1:2-4) Or will they bring condemnation?

Job said in his sufferings, "I loathe my own life; I will give full vent to my complaint; I will speak in the bitterness of my soul, I will say to God, 'Do not condemn me. . .'" (Job 10:1,2). Before we quickly criticize Job's words, let us remind ourselves that we have *never* suffered as he did!! Also, God said that Job did not sin, even in his complaints—for there was no need at the end of the book to have a sacrifice made for Job's sins. And that wonderful thought makes me also snuggle down in my spiritual blanket. Whatever this suffering I am experiencing, it is nothing like Job's, and I sing, "He is able to deliver thee. Though by sin opprest, go to Him for rest; 'Our God is able to deliver thee.'"

My Meditation Shall Be Sweet

"My meditation of him shall be sweet: I will be glad in the Lord" (Psalm 104:34) KJV. Why will it be sweet? One reason is because of our "one hope." I shall live with Him one day. This present suffering will pass, or if it doesn't, I am going home. Paul tells us that going home is the better of the two. And the song, " 'Tis so sweet to trust in Jesus, just to take Him at this word. Just to rest upon His promise, just to say, 'Thus saith the Lord.' "

This is sweet. Where is that pain that awakened me? It is muted. It is lessened. There are more important things than sleeping, and one of them is growing spiritually. *The value of sufferings needs to be ap-*

preciated. These pains are given and used by God for our good. I wouldn't have missed tonight for anything!

I close this chapter rather reluctantly. It is such a short one. I close it with the pain from the arthritis subsiding. A vestige of a black eye from a previous, dangerous fall still lingers. (Even that fall worked together for good, as it reassured me that God wasn't through with me and my work for Him!)

I go back to bed not anticipating the closing of my eyes in rest, but "hyper" over what I have learned tonight. Finally, I have partially understood why He gives us those songs in the night. It is probably when we cannot sleep because of pain that our souls seek out the Comforter, the Father, and our Pilot. "Jesus, Savior, pilot me, over life's tempestuous sea. Unknown waves before me roll, hiding rocks and treacherous shoals. . . ."

Another truth has been revealed, another piece of the puzzle of life is found. I can say, truly, "Thank you for the pain. It was more than worth that little pain for the sweet songs that came—in the night."

Sweet Songs In The Night

In the quiet of the night while the household sleeps
My pain awakes me and I am prone to weep.
But gradually my thoughts take me away
To my loving Father—and I pray.
He hears me, He sees me, He lessens my pain,
And I smile at the words of familiar strains,
Beautiful songs oft come to mind.
And sleep is never far behind.

Lea Fowler

QUESTIONS FOR DISCUSSIONS

1. Why do we seek Him in the night?

2. Have you learned to meditate?

3. How does relief increase our faith?

UNREQUITED LOVE
Chapter 11 ✓

"What the world needs now, is love, sweet love," a popular song says, and it is certainly true. It is also what the church needs, too. Many families lack love, and many individuals must walk past lighted windows and wish someone, somewhere was waiting for them. Dale Carnegie tells of a famous Russian writer, I think it was Tolstoy, who said something like this, "I would give all my fame and wealth in exchange for some woman who was waiting supper for me and cared if I was late."

God is love. Every factor of love makes up His being and through His love, He sent us a Savior to show us what God was like, what love is, and to reveal His plan for our joining Him when this life is over. Part of His will was for us, who are naturally "unlovely," "children of wrath," to lose that old cocoon of sin and begin to look and think like God.

But, often we feel unloved, unwanted, unappreciated by our fellow-man, even by the brethren. So, let's talk about this awhile and pray that God will give us the needed answers and understanding when things don't go right, especially in matters of the heart.

Puppy Love

Can make you as "sick as a dog." Too many adults forget how it feels to have a "crush" on one of the opposite sex. I am an incurable romantic, and there was a score of names through the years who caused my young heart to beat faster. (Very few, if any, reciprocated the same feeling!)

Little girls play dolls and play house and yearn for the day when they get to be a beautiful bride in that lovely, white dress. However, not many little boys are interested in the same things; they are busy getting dirty and chasing girls with bugs and snakes.

But, in the teenager years, when puppy loves begins to bloom in both sexes, the heartbreak often starts. Those in the know tell us that

55

a boy reaches the peak of his sexual desires at 17! (This causes panic not only in the minds of the mothers who know their daughter is the object of his affection, but also in the minds of the mothers of the sons.)

In this day of casual sex, scary statistics of failed teenager marriages and the alarming rate of abortions and unwanted pregnancies, we realize we need all the help we can get to guide them into a safe harbor. To wait for the young man or woman they will love when they are an adult.

In my day, it was expected for the father to marry the girl who was carrying his baby, no matter his or her age. The decent thing to do was to have a quick marriage. But, this custom is rapidly changing, that of forcing two children into marriage. Many good and innocent parents are realizing that they *can bear the shame* and can see their daughter or son through this terrible time in their lives. Some help raise the new baby; some encourage the girl to let the child be adopted by Christian parents.

What am I suggesting? This is a hard decision. One that needs a lot of prayer and maturity on the part of the adults involved. The parents, the preacher, and the relatives often make a hasty decision, not looking for the best interests of the young couple or the child. I would just say this—consider the probability of a future divorce. We might even lose our child who marries an unbeliever! The church should find in themselves forgiveness and mercy if repentance sought. Don't force a baby to marry a baby to have a baby.

And often the end result is many tears, whatever the decision. The "puppy love" very seldom lasts or grows into maturity. MARRIAGE IS FOR ADULTS AND EVEN THEN, IT IS DIFFICULT.

The Breakup Of Engagements

In the time of the birth of Jesus, it was the custom for each family to select a marriage partner for their children when they were young. In fact, even if there was no marriage, just an engagement, there had to be a divorce at the breakup of the alliance. If you remember, Joseph was going to put Mary away quietly so as to not disgrace her. There was no consummation of their love until after their marriage and the birth of Jesus. "And Joseph rose from his sleep, and did as the angel of the Lord commanded him, and took her as his wife, and kept her a virgin until she gave birth to a Son, and he called his name Jesus" (Matthew 1:23-25).

Our customs are different today. An engagement *should* mean, "We are or think we are in love. We plan to marry on this set date."

But, there are changed minds and circumstances. The sending of the invitations or the buying of the gown should not cause the wrong decision to be made. What a travesty or tragedy to go ahead and marry the wrong person just because of embarrassment, or completed wedding preparations, or most important of all, going against one's own good judgment! We have all seen this happen many times, and we have all witnessed the heartbreak, divorce, or a loveless marriage. It is never too late to break off the engagement—even if the music has begun!

Parents should get their pride out of the way if the marriage is called off! Happiness is what we should want for our sons and daughters. Not only their happiness but also for God's approval of their choice of mate. The motive for the Christian bride and groom should be for a "once in a lifetime" marriage—not just an exciting wedding!

College should be secured for the groom or a way to make an adequate living for his wife and children. She should be trained to help from the home, if necessary. All of these matters should be taught to our children from the cradle—up.

Teach it right—even if they don't do it right! "Marry in haste and repent at leisure" is still a truism. Don't "tell" your children what is right but "teach" them. If they decide to go against their training, you have the comfort of knowing that the choice was theirs, and the blame not yours.

How To Endure A Lost Love

Someone has said, "One truth I hold, I hold when I sorrow most, 'tis better to have loved and lost than never to have loved at all." I agree with that. All kinds of love exist around us. Lasting love, fighting love, untrue love, possessive love, neglecting love, and growing love.

Love involves pain sooner or later. An old song says, "A song of love is a sad song." And it is. While we love, we are vulnerable. The more we love, the more vulnerable we are! Who was it that said, "The course of true love never runs smoothly."? Shakespeare, I believe.

To me, one of the saddest love songs of all is when loves comes to an older woman for the first time and ends wrong. What do you say to help heal her broken heart? Emotions have been awakened for the first time, even temptations burn within the mind and body as she is pursued. She is tempted to go against her principles and godly life.

But yet, after it is all a memory and the acute sufferings have faded, should she hate the "monster" who so misused her or will the memories, in time, enrich her life? Won't it make her more understanding with others as they suffer? Won't the love of yesterday soften her heart and the time come when she can truly feel "this too, worked together for my good'"? I guess this depends on who she is, how badly she was hurt, and how much time has passed.

If You But Knew

If you but knew
How all my days seemed filled with dreams of you,
How sometimes in the silent night
Yours eyes thrill through me with their tender light,
How oft I hear your voice when others speak,
How you 'mid others form I seek—
Oh, love more real than through such dreams were
     true
If you but knew.

Could you but guess
How you alone make all my happiness,
How I am more than willing for your sake
To stand alone, give all and nothing take,
Nor chafe to think you bound while I am free,
Quite free, till death, to love you silently,
Could you but guess.

Could you but learn
How when you doubt my truth I sadly yearn
To tell you all, to stand for one brief space
Unfettered, soul to soul, as face to face,
To crown you king, my king, till life shall end,
My lover, and likewise my truest friend,
Would you love me, dearest, as fondly in return,
Could you but learn?

UNKNOWN

The Deepest Cut Of All

God tells us about it in Malachi 2:13-17. "And this is another thing you do: you cover the altar of the LORD with tears, with weeping and with groaning because he no longer regards the offering or accepts it with favor from your hand. Yet you say, 'For what reason?' Because the LORD has been a witness between you and the wife of your youth, against whom you have dealt treacherously, though she is your companion and your wife, by covenant. But not one has done so who has a remnant of the Spirit. And what did that one do while he was seeking a godly offerspring? Take heed then, to your spirit, and let no one deal treacherously against the wife of your youth. For I hate divorce, says the LORD, the God of Israel, and him who covers his garment with wrong, says the LORD of hosts. So take heed to your spirit, that you do not deal treacherously. You have wearied the LORD with your words. Yet you say, 'How have we wearied him?' In that you say, 'Everyone who does evil is good in the sight of the LORD, and he delights in them, 'Or, 'Where is the God of justice?' "

God tells men who have put away the wives of their youth that He does not want their offerings. He calls them treacherous, for she was their companion and wife by covenant—by a vow. "You have wearied me for you say that God delights in this evil." And the Lord is saying, "I hate divorce."

Can you imagine, women of God, the horror of receiving a letter from your husband, saying that you have been put away? The home is no longer yours; the children are no longer yours, and there is no place to go. Many women of the long ago experienced such cruelty by men who proclaimed to be God fearing. Though we do not live under such a system today, nevertheless, many Christian women—older and younger—are put away heartlessly and exchanged for a younger spouse.

I have spent hours listening to broken-hearted women, grandmothers, weeping for their husbands, hoping they will come back to them. They seldom do. (Probably a lot of them wish they could return later on.) It is harder for an older man to adjust to his younger wife and her ways than he once thought. He misses his comfortable home, his family, and his grandchildren. Things are never right for him again. The scars will ever remain—even if there is a reconciliation.

Fidelis

You have taken back the promise
That you spoke so long ago;
Taken back the heart you gave me—
I must let it go.
Where Love once has breathed, Pride dieth,
So, I struggled, but in vain;
First to keep the links together,
Then to piece the broken chain. . . . .

Adelaide Proctor

Taken from "The Best Loved Poems of
The American People"

How Does The Survivor Survive?

Just as any other Christian sufferer survives. God, Jesus, the Scriptures, the brethren, and time. Let us not leave out The Comforter.

Jesus promised that we would not be left orphans but that He would send the Comforter. "And I will ask the Father, and He will give you another Helper (Comforter) that He may be with your forever;. . . . . .I will not leave you as orphans; I will come to you" (John 14:16,19).

Really, the one who suffers most and is healed, truly appreciates the power of the Godhead. "Come unto me and I will give you rest," God whispers to us through His Son.

The Great Physician

The wound will close though the scars remain.
The clouds will pass, you will smile again.
God holds your heart within His hands
And He knows how much pain you can withstand.
The Great Physician ne'er leaves His post
And is ever there when you need Him most.

Lea Fowler

QUESTIONS FOR STUDY

1. Did the disciples or apostles ever turn their backs on Jesus?
   Yes

2. The Church is called the bride of Christ. Is His bride always faithful? *No*

3. How does Jesus feel about the unfaithful bride?
   Sad; wants the unfaithful to be truly sorrowful and repent.

THE LOSS OF A LOVED ONE
Chapter 12

To All Parents

I'll lend you for a little while a child of mine," he said. "For you to love the while he lives and mourn for when he's dead. It may be six or seven years or twenty-two or three. But will you, till I call him back, take care of him for me? He'll bring his charms to gladden you, and should his stay be brief, you'll have his lovely memories as solace for your grief."

"I cannot promise he will stay, since all from earth return but there are lessons taught down there I want this child to learn. I've searched the wide world over in my search for teachers' true and from the throngs that crowd life's lanes I have selected you. Now, will you give him all your love nor think the labor vain; nor hate me when I come to take him back again?"

"I fancied that I heard them say, 'Dear Lord, Thy will be done. For all the joy this child shall bring, the risk of grief we'll run. We'll shelter him with happiness; we'll love while we may. And for the happiness we've known, forever grateful stay, but should the angels call for him sooner than we'd plan, we'll brave the bitter grief that comes and try to understand.' "

Edgar Guest

The Loss Of A Child

Is there any heartbreak like losing a child? The mother in me says, "No." We went through the "valley of the shadow of death" with a small daughter and with a grown one. God, in His mercy, delivered them both and us! I'll never forget the panic, the grief, the attempt to pray with a "large brick" in my throat, the feeling *no one understood* and the desperate longing to talk to a mother who did understand— one who had lost a child.

When we came to worship after we returned home with our little girl, an older mother of many children touched my shoulder as we sat

61

down. I don't remember her name, but I do remember what she said. "I know how you feel today. I've taken them to the hospital and didn't bring them back. And I also remember how it feels to bring them home again!"

Oh, what a ministry she had to offer, and she offered it that day to me, mother who had been assured by many doctors that there was no hope for her child. *But there was hope.* For, she lives today and the grown daughter, too. *God has the last diagnosis and prescription!* Elders had come and prayed; the whole church prayed—even the whole little city seemed to be praying.

At times like this, call in the righteous, for God hears their prayers! My husband and I had prayed together and had resolved together to let them go, if that was to be the final result. And to pick up the pieces of our lives and live faithfully, knowing we would be with them in eternity.

Mark your Bibles in 2 Samuel 12:21-23. "Then his servants said to him, 'What is this thing that you have done? While the child was alive, you fasted and wept; but when the child died, you arose and ate food.' And he said, 'While the child was still alive, I fasted and wept; for I said, Who knows, the Lord may be gracious to me that the child may live but now he has died; why should I fast? Can I bring him back again? I shall go to him but he will not return to me.' "

You will need to remember where this is found. For you will need to share it with many grieving parents after the loss of their child. Whether they are religious people or not; they *need* to know what God says here.

An Interview With A Mother

This young mother is a neighbor of the local preacher's wife. She is busy serving in her community, her family, her church. She is involved in all kinds of children's activities. She and her husband now have two beautiful children, a boy and a girl.

But, they lost their first child, Jeremy, when he was 6 years old. He was killed in a bicycle accident. A little neighbor child had come running and calling her—"Your little boy is hurt; he's hurt bad." That afternoon the parents had a few things to do before the three would go for ice-cream. It was suggested that the child ride down to the corner store and when he returned, they would leave together.

A Flashback

While this baby was growing under his mother's heart, her husband was serving in Vietnam. Her own mother, who was only 43, whom she loved fiercely, had died and the baby was due.

What a time to have a baby, and especially a first one! A husband away in the terrible ordeal of war with the daily worries of whether he was safe, whether he would return. And the traumatic experience of losing her beloved mother. What a time of suffering and yet what joy in the birth of her first child! Alone—and yet blessed with her baby. No longer alone.

The husband returned alive, and they rejoiced in the child.

The Folly Of Well-Meaning Friends

People need to be more careful at such a time as this. She still remembers unthinking remarks like: "I don't know how it feels to lose a child, but why did you let him ride a bike?"

"Well, he is with the angels." (That thought would be comforting some day but not while her arms are so empty.)

"This is God's will." (How can anyone know that?)

Guilt overwhelmed them at this time. Even their lawyer had advised them not to pursue a lawsuit because they might be branded negligent, even though they were not.

Strain On The Marriage

Statistics bear out that many marriages do not survive the death of a child, especially an accidental death.

Their reactions were normal and typical. The father hurt so much that he couldn't talk about it. She thought about nothing else and could talk nothing else. She could not stay out of Jeremy's room.

It was suggested by relatives that they should get away for awhile. So, they started off together, hoping to lessen the present pain and recapture their love and peace of mind. They drove up into the beautiful Blue Ridge Mountains, stopped the van and looked out at God's handiwork. Both of them, at the same time, were tempted to just drive on off the cliff. It would be an instant way out for their unbearable pain—but they couldn't do it. They still could not talk but got out of the van and sat for hours, grieving.

Her Faith

"Did it hurt your faith?" I asked. She answered, "I was afraid you would ask that." It did—for a while. So much tragedy at once would be hard for older people and certainly for younger ones. She stopped attending church; her heart hardened within her at the thought: "God could have kept it from happening but didn't."

Hopefully, in time, all of us realize that God sets up the laws of nature. A man who jumps off a high building will suffer the same fate as the toddler who stumbles off. Human nature makes us run toward the protection of a tree during a storm but wisdom should teach us to run from a tree, as trees are lightning rods.

This loss of faith was only temporary. The healing process brought back her relationship with God, and she is faithful once again.

The Hardest Times Now

Birthdays, Christmas, the anniversary of his death. The worst day of all? Mother's Day. Every year, Mother's Day. The pain, the vacancy, will always be there.

Along the Road

I walked a mile with Pleasure
She chattered all the way
But left me none the wiser
For all she had to say.

I walked a mile with Sorrow
And ne'er a word said she;
But oh, the things I learned from her
When Sorrow walked with me.

Robert Hamilton

(From The Best Loved Poems of
the American People)

The Loss Of A Husband

If I were a widow, this would be the chapter I would read first. Will there be something said that will comfort my loneliness? If so, it will probably be said by another widow.

There are more and more women who have lost their companions. The two are no longer one, just one, alone, now. Someone has said, "When the two become one and the other one is not with them, they are half a person." All of us have felt like a half-person when we were experiencing an unusual joy or excitement and away from our mates. We longed to share the occasion with them.

Death has a finality about it that has its own peculiar comfort, intertwined with pain. No matter the consolation given, the kindnesses shown, our inner self knows that a chapter is over. I remember an old man coming to a new widow and saying, "Death is hard to get acquainted with." And it is.

While our loved one is still alive, there are constant anxieties and fear of the unknown. There is still hope—and fervent prayer for a miraculous reversal of his or her condition. But, when death comes, no longer are we in the fluid state, but certainities of what lies ahead begin to form.

We need to rise up like David did when he lost his child. The fasting is over; the clothes are to be changed; we worship again and we eat again. Life starts over.

Death

The bustle in a House
The morning after Death
Is Solemnest of industries
Enacted upon earth—
The sweeping up the Heart
And putting Love away
We shall not want to use again
Until eternity.

Anon.

In the preceding section of this chapter, the statement was made, "Surely there is nothing worse than losing a child." But the friend that was with me in the hospital at the near death of our child said, "Yes, losing a husband would be worse. You can have other children, but your mate cannot be replaced." I have thought of that remark many times.

An Interview

This couple had a short engagement but a long marriage. They were married 42 years. "We got acquainted after marriage," she told me. They had two children, a son and a daughter. But, they loved young people, and teenagers continued to congregate in their home and yard after their children were grown.

She is a strong women, a self-sufficient lady. After her husband's death, she felt she could not let down, that she couldn't afford to go to pieces—because she might not regain her former ground. "No one knows how bad it is (death) until they experience it. It is inexpressible, the pain, the agony, as you are forced to let them go." But, she wouldn't bring him back, not as he was. But would as he used to be.

Her husband, who was a diabetic—carefully controlled, had a car wreck and was never well again. He died 8 months after the accident.

He was a great kidder; he would say things like, "I'd be worth more dead than alive." She would answer, "I'll take you just as you are." They did a lot of entertaining, and he loved to cook out in their backyard. He loved his mother, and this was reflected in his concern for older widows. He was always repairing the homes of widows because, "There is no man around the house."

A Widow's Advice

1. "Get involved in your finances!" He handled every aspect of the checkbook so she wouldn't be "bothered" with it. He was generous with her. He gave her everything she needed and wanted. He sur-

65

rounded her with all the luxuries he could provide. But, he handicapped her, unintentionally, by not involving her in the finances of the home.

2. "After your husband dies, keep your home. There should be no sudden change in life-style or location."

3. "Have women friends now and stay close to your family."

4. "Remember the beautiful memories. Try not to suffer over what could have been—emphasize the positives not the negatives. You will delay your recovery if you don't do this."

The Effect On Her Faith

When I asked her, "Did you blame God?" She answered very emphatically, "Never! Never! I have never wondered, 'Why, me?' for I look around and I see so many others who are much worse off than me. It gave me comfort to know that he would not have been happy to have been house-bound."

He was a talker, a former car salesman, and an outdoor man who loved his horses, a gregarious man who enjoyed people.

The Saturday before he died, they had a big barbecue, and most of the church was there. He helped cook and serve. Someone asked later, "Did this occasion hasten his death?" "He was doing what he wanted to do!" was her answer.

Today she answers, "Would I bring him back? To sickness and new hurts? No. He wouldn't have wanted that."

Her faith has increased through her sufferings. She thanks God every day for what she has. "I realize what I have is the Lord's, and I pray for wisdom to handle it rightly."

How Can We Help Her?

Include her every time we think of it. Make times to involve her in eating out with the girls or get togethers at someone's home. We need to remember the principle to do unto others as we would be done by. She remarked to me, "In being single, you are not included in many things you would enjoy—because you are single." *Shame on us! And shame on me!*

What Is Her Life Today?

She is such an example of bravery to the rest of us. Her husband would be so proud of her, I'm sure. There are some widows who "die" when their husbands do—but this one lives and serves others.

Her life is the church and her family. She wants to live as long as she can. "Why grieve your life away when you can help others?"

She misses her husband, especially when the bass voices lead out in the song, "Lead Me Gently Home, Father," for he sang bass.

She comforts herself with this thought: *"We are both alive though separated—separated, but on hold."*

The Loss Of A Mother

Nobody's Child

Suddenly you were old,
I thought it would be a gradual thing
Not on a certain day, at a given moment.
The watch I kept was through the eye of self,
Veiled by the vision of time, not your own.
Evening shadows gathered around you
While I was looking at tomorrow,
Now you've turned a corner where
I cannot follow—leaving me behind
And nobody's child.

Author Unknown

I did not know my mother—hardly remember anything about her—wouldn't remember her beautiful face, except for pictures. She died when I was nine years old, after a long sickness.

But, I am still conscious of the void in my life created by her absence. I know she loved her children. I've always missed her and always will.

Sometimes I feel that void has grown deeper through the years because of the closeness I have with my own children. They are my best friends—as is my husband. I have never known "that best friend," the one whom I could turn to in security and love as my children turn to me.

A 75 year old woman said to me last night, "I miss my mother so much. I wish she was here to tell me what to do."

My father was wonderful—the best father in the world, but he couldn't be my mother.

An Interview With A Daughter

This daughter was the "middle child." There were three girls and one boy in the family. Her mother was industrious at 16, for at 18 she had saved enough money to buy a house. She continued to work after marriage and motherhood. But, the children were never at home without a parent. (Only a close, family friend or relative was used as an occasional sitter.)

While she was at home, she read Bible stories to the children and prayed with them, too. On her days off, she took them to enjoyable places. On pay day, she brought all four children a gift. So, the daughter's memories are not of a deprived child, though her mother worked away from home for a time.

The mother converted her husband, and he went to a seminary to learn how to preach for a living. Then, she stopped working away from home because there would have been no parent with the children. When the children started school, the mother was there! She always wanted to know what they were learning. She checked their papers daily and was involved with their education.

Their home was filled with songs, all kinds of songs. Not only were there songs, but also there was lots of laughter. Her father was very strict and did not allow any laughing at the table. But, mother would often get them tickled; the father would send them to their room—and mother would feed them later.

They moved often, but the daughter looks at these moves as good things in her life. She learned to make friends easily. They never *had to move* during the school year.

Discipline In The Home

How did the parents punish these children? Dad was a disciplinarian; mother used a switch. But, the discipline continued by both parents to the four children at all ages. The daughter still thinks that her parents were too strict. She was not allowed to spend a night away from home at a girl-friend's, but she could have girl-friends come to her home. (She did not allow her own children to spend nights away from home, either!)

When I ask, "Did she talk to you a lot?" She answered, "She wanted to, but it seemed there was always someone around." (That is a PK's—Preacher's Kids-common complaint. A house full of others burdened with *their* needs.)

"Did you ever push her to the limit—threaten to leave—to rebel?"

"No. I always knew she meant what she said. I never dared to go beyond."

This daughter remained a faithful Christian. Some of the others did not. When the mother wondered why this had happened, she comforted herself with the hope that they would all come back to the Lord someday.

On each Monday the mother started preparing for the approaching Sunday. Sunday was the most important day of the week to her, yet even with this example, it became just another day to those who fell away.

This daughter went home often. Her husband and children were very close to the grandparents. The other grown children did not come home often. (They could have felt uncomfortable because of their unfaithfulness.)

The Death Of Her Mother

Her mother had always felt that she would die at 68, and she had a massive heart attack at this age. Though the daughter was with the mother at this crucial time, she was not with her during her last moments, for she died suddenly.

There is no doubt in the daughter's mind that they will spend eternity together and sing together the new songs and laugh together again. (Without interruptions.)

Why did I ask *this* lady to talk to me about her mother? Because I knew she *really loved* her mother in a special way. Because each Lord's Day, the most important day of the week (by training and example) brings her mother back to her. In a way, she meets her mother as well as her Lord each Lord's Day.

She said "I cry during the singing often. I can't sing 'Amazing Grace'—ever. And there are phrases in many songs that I can't sing in thinking of her."

A song comes to my mind as I close this chapter—a song applying to our families. "Will The Circle Be Unbroken, By and By, By and By?" That is probably the last thought of a Christian mother as she closes her eyes on earth.

A Final Blow or Victory

Death will come in time to all,
Will we be prepared when it comes to call?
Will we greet it as a friend or foe—
In happiness—or in bitter woe?
The decision belongs to you and me
A final blow or a victory!

Lea Fowler

QUESTIONS FOR DISCUSSION

1. What can we learn through David's loss of a child?

2. Why is a husband's death so hard to bear?

3. What is a Christian mother's greatest hope?

THE LAST SUFFERING
Chapter 13

"We are born in another's suffering and die in our own," someone once said. We don't know how or when we will leave this old world. (And aren't we blessed to not know!) But, if Jesus doesn't come back in our lifetime, then the only way we get out of here is to die.

Most Christians theoretically look forward to heaven. We recognize our "one hope" is to live eternally with Him. But most of us don't want *today* to be the last day. Someday, but not today. I heard a man say at church, "If the bus came in today, I'd take a later bus!"

Yet God pronounces a blessing on those who are ready today—those who even *wish* that today would be the day of His coming.

"Now there is in store for me the crown of righteousness, which the Lord, the righteous Judge, will award to me on that day—and not only to me, but also to all who have longed for his appearing" (2 Timothy 4:8) NIV

". . . . .and not just to me, but to all those whose lives show that they are eagerly looking forward to his coming back again." LB

". . . .and not only to me, but to all those who wait with love for him to appear." TEV

The scriptures are full of admonitions to Christians and to the world that He is coming back and we are to be ready.

"Be dressed in readiness, and keep your lamps alight. And be like men who are waiting for their master when he returns from the wedding feast, so that they may immediately open the door to him when he comes and knocks. Blessed are those slaves whom the master shall find on the alert when he comes; truly I say to you, that he will gird himself to serve, and have them recline at table, and will come up and wait on them. . . . .You, too, be ready; for the Son of Man is coming at an hour you do not expect" (Luke 12:35-37,40).

God Sees Death Differently

He sees the clouds from the inside, the silver lining. He knows that death to the saved is entering a much more beautiful home, one from which we would never choose to leave!

We say, "We like it here," and He answers, "You'll love it there." Isn't it peculiar that believers hold on to the present life with its troubles, anxieties, pain, tears, and temptations rather than holding on to God's hand as He wipes away our tears and memories of the unhappy past?

"For behold, I create new heavens and a new earth; and the former things shall not be remembered or come to mind" (Isaiah 65:17).

"And he shall wipe away every tear from their eyes; and there shall no longer be any death; there shall no longer be any mourning, or crying, or pain; the first things have passed away" (Revelations 21:4).

Is God Happy About Every Death?

The babies, the children, the mentally retarded are safe. "For of such is the kingdom of God." I am sure He is happy to greet each of them. I used to be concerned for this group when I thought of them perishing in the time of Noah, and then I realized had the children grown to maturity, they would probably have become like their wicked parents!

But God tells us how he hates the death of His grown children who know the truth and won't obey it. Ezekiel 33:11 says, "Say to them, 'As I live!' declares the Lord God, 'I take no pleasure in the death of the wicked, but rather that the wicked turn from his way and live. Turn back, turn back from your evil ways! Why then will you die, O house of Israel?' "

How foolish for a *believer* to be lost eternally! John 3:16 tells us that a "believer *should* not perish," not "*shall* not perish." An unbeliever is condemned already (John 3:18). John 3:36 tells us that belief and obedience *are both necessary* for salvation! Many believers quit reading too soon. "A disciple is one who believes His teachings, rests upon His sacrifice, imbibes His spirit, and walks in His steps." Farrar

Why Do We Dread Death?

One reason is pain. Who wants to hurt so badly that they die? Do *all* die in great pain? No. Many pass away in their sleep. Many die instantly in accidents. Many are kept under sedatives until they slip away.

I think it is interesting to read some of the studies made concerning death. The investigators interview people who have seemingly died—by drowning, by the heart stopping, and so forth. And the recovered victims do not usually recount a lot of fear or pain after they are revived. In fact, many of them did not want to come back and had to force themselves to re-enter this world.

Death literally means separation. We dread losing our loved ones, and they dread losing us. Seldom are we ready to let them go.

71

The Sting Of Death

The sting of death is sin. "The sting of death is sin, and the power of sin is the law; but thanks be to God, who gives us the victory through our Lord Jesus Christ. Therefore my beloved brethren, be steadfast, immovable, always abounding in the work of the Lord, knowing that your toil is not in vain in the Lord" (1 Corinthians 15:56-58). Try to forget your longing for the deceased *who die in the Lord.* They are safe. They just went ahead a little ways and are around the bend. They wouldn't choose to come back if they could—and they can't. Let them go in peace through your love and faith.

As for those who die in unbelief, that's God's business. "For what have I to do with judging outsiders? Do you not judge those within the church but those who are outside, God judges. . . . . ." (1 Corinthians 5:12,13). They are in the hands of a merciful God who weighs their past thoughts and actions.

God gives all responsible people the right of choice to where they will spend eternity. We must do the same. "Do not feel personally responsible for everything. That's My job. Love, God." Anon.

"But we do not want you to be uninformed, brethren, about those who are asleep, that you may not grieve, as do the rest who have no hope. For if we believe that Jesus died and rose again, even so God will bring with him those who have fallen asleep in Jesus. . . . . . .Then we who are alive and remain shall be caught up together with them in the clouds to meet the Lord in the air, and thus we shall always be with the Lord. Therefore comfort one another with these words" (1 Thessalonians 4:13,14,17,18).

Seminars On Death

Jerry Hill of the Timothy Hill Boy's Ranch in New York holds seminars on death and dying. I was privileged to attend one. They are wonderful, and we need more of them!

The word "death" strikes fear in all of us. These words: terminal, critical, pneumonia, cancer, heart attack, emphysema, etc. do the same thing. But God would have His faithful people look at those words with understanding and acceptance. He would have us be calm in the eye of the storm.

God's Promise To The Dying Christian

"Precious in the sight of the Lord is the death of his godly ones" (Psalm 116:15). What does that mean to you? To me, it means we "won't have to cross Jordan alone." A familiar song has the phrase, "He'll hold my hand while I am dying." It means He will not give me more than I can bear at the last. It means I can trust Him to my final breath—that He will send the angels for me—and take me to Paradise.

72

We either believe this or we don't. If we don't believe it now—hopefully we will grow to believe it. A good friend of mine didn't use to believe there was a heaven. But she suffered much pain, she grew in the Lord, and now as we talk together, we await together His coming to take us home to heaven. God isn't through with us yet. (My family will be saying now, "She is happy, Mama. We're all crying." As my son-in-law once said at a family reunion, "Let's never play that game again where we all cry.")

Funerals

Christian funerals are gradually changing for the better, it seems to me. Congregational singing has become more common. The songs are more joyful. Instead of, "We're going down the valley one by one" which always aroused both fear and laughter in me, we're beginning to sing songs like "O Happy Day," "My Hope Is Built On Nothing Less," "Hallelujah, We Shall Rise," "Won't It Be Wonderful There," and "Beulah Land."

No Funeral Gloom

No funeral gloom, my dears, when I am gone,
Corpse gazings, tears, black raiment, graves and
*   grimness.*
Think of me as withdrawn into the dimness,
Yours still, you mine.
Remember all the best of our past moments
And forget the rest.
And so to where I walk come gently on.

Ellen Terry

(From *The Best Loved Poems of the American People*)

Russ and I have our cemetery lots. They are beautiful. We pass them often and remark, "There's where our bodies will rest for awhile after we go HOME." And it gives us joy and peace to realize we'll rest together and rise together after the Spirit gives life to our mortal bodies. "But if the Spirit of him who raised Jesus from the dead dwells in you, he who raised Christ Jesus from the dead will also give life to your mortal bodies, through his Spirit who indwells you" (Romans 8:11).

May this chapter—and this book—comfort you "when you suffer."

Earth Without Rain

Suffering is a part of God's plan
For a better life—to understand
That a life without pain is

73

Like earth without rain.
That flowers bloom where there
Once was doom.
When this life is done and
The battles are won—
It's only then we'll really see
That the end of the page brought victory.

Lea Fowler

QUESTIONS FOR DISCUSSION

1. Why do we fear death? *The unknown* *death; then death.*
   I fear the pain and sickness before the *moved the death.*
2. What did Jesus look forward to after death and how does this relate
   to us? *Living with God his Father. If we are saved we*
   can live with in heaven also.
3. Do you know of a Christian who died calmly and in faith?

SUGGESTIONS FOR FURTHER CLASS STUDY

There are some chapters that can be subdivided. This book should be
able to be extended another 6 weeks if used for class study. Go at your
own speed, but don't hurry.

Books To Read

The Problem of Pain by *C.S. Lewis*
Straight Talk To Men and Their Wives by *Dr. James Dobson*
Also, books by Leo Busgalia and Max Lucado are recommended.